COMPUTERIZED SHIPPING SYSTEMS:

INCREASING PROFIT AND PRODUCTIVITY THROUGH TECHNOLOGY

NEW MILLENIUM EDITION

Mark A. Taylor

Computerized Shipping Systems:
INCREASING PROFIT AND
PRODUCTIVITY THROUGH TECHNOLOGY
New Millennium Edition
Mark A. Taylor

Angelico & Taylor, Inc.
Plymouth, Michigan

Library of Congress Information
Shipment of goods -- Data processing.
HF5761.T39 2000 698921

Editors: Dr. David F. Stein/Don Tanner
Cover & Book Design: Michael Haines
Illustrations/Graphics: John Edwards

Address inquiries to:
Angelico & Taylor, Inc.
40800 Five Mile Road
Plymouth, MI 48170

ISBN 0-9648365-1-7
2nd Printing
Printed in the United States of America

To my best friend and partner in life;
Vera, my beloved wife.

Acknowledgments

I have had a great deal of help and advice from many people in writing this book. I would like to thank the following individuals who were especially helpful including: Dr. David Stein who laboriously and expertly edited my material, Michael Haines for his design and formatting work, Don Tanner and Steve Lipsen who managed the details to make it happen, Robert Malley, Aaron Dones and all of my account managers for their views and comments, Christina Champion, my mother, for proofreading the book and Vera Angelico, my wife, for her never ending encouragement and support.

Table of Contents

Table of Contents (continued)

Table of Contents *(continued)*

Preface

The computerized shipping systems business has evolved rapidly over the last 15 years, driven by the carriers and their constantly changing compliance requirements, innovations in technology, and customer realization of the impact the shipping department has on the organization. The globalization of world markets, the trend toward supply chain management, the implementation of enterprise software and the growth of the Internet and e-commerce have all made tremendous impacts on the way we conduct business — and our competitiveness and profitability.

The industry was born in the mid-1980's and developed concurrently with the personal computer. In the beginning, shipping systems could weigh packages, convert zip codes to zones, and produce manifests. Shipping history was archived on floppy disks. As the PC changed, so did its functionality for shipping. The invention of the hard drive allowed for storage of customer databases and the printing of address labels. When networks became a reality, so did the possibility of multiple users and connecting the shipping department to a business information system. As new carriers entered the market, more, and more complex, services were created. Rate shopping was born. And as the carriers created compliance requirements and special bar coded labels, thermal printers were introduced. We can predict that as technology changes, so will shipping systems.

Since computer technology, both hardware and software, as well as carrier compliance requirements are rapidly changing, there is a constant drive to upgrade or replace systems. Customer growth and changing business conditions are among the principal reasons for adopting a computerized shipping system. The best ones are provided by independent consultants and vendors (not the major carriers) and I will demonstrate many times in this book why that is so. Let's face it, this is an era for small parcel shipment, spurred on by increasing emphasis on just-in-time shipments and supply chain management, as well as the growth of E-commerce. Just think of how many parcels most of us get at home each week.

I have written this book to teach managers, business owners and other professional consultants what is possible through technology in the shipping department: how computerized shipping systems can reduce freight costs, increase productivity, and improve customer and employee satisfaction. Far too often, I have seen shipping and operations managers suffer after making hasty or uninformed purchase decisions, ones that end up costing thousands of dollars. The culprit is usually a new system that didn't work as promised, lacked the required flexibility and connectivity, or quickly became obsolete.

A Vision

I have devoted the last ten years to getting the word out—in person and in print—about what is possible with computerized shipping systems. I truly care because I hate to see waste. I hate to see people being misled, manipulated and sold a bill of goods. I hate hearing managers say, "If I had only understood my options, I could have done better." I hate it because the same thing has happened to me in my own business life.

I also see a cynicism and a distrust of technology on the part of decision makers that bothers me, yet I know that it has been earned in many cases. I am tired of seeing people misinformed and then taken advantage of. Worse yet, I don't think the false promises have been intentional. As one of my favorite jokes goes, "Do you know the difference between the snake oil salespersons in the days of the Old West and many of today's high technology salespersons?" The snake oil hawkers knew when they were lying—when their product couldn't deliver on its promises.

So, my second hope is that those who sell computerized shipping systems will read this book and learn from it. I envision sales people educating shipping and operations managers, as a means to new relationships of respect and mutual benefit.

Trusting Technology

I was one of the launch managers of the very first computerized shipping system and, since then, have pioneered the introduction and development of computers in shipping rooms across America. Now, twenty-five years later, I am proud to say that I have visited and studied (and helped improve) more than 10,000 shipping departments.

I can also say that I believe in what technology, properly applied, can do to free mankind of drudgery, while increasing productivity and self-esteem. As I've indicated already, it is perhaps sometimes too convenient to express a distrust in technology, when the fault lies in ourselves and in our understanding and implementation of it.

Technology can increase productivity by making business processes faster, easier, and more accurate. In the shipping room, it can eliminate tedious, error-prone manual labor; cut waste; improve communications; enhance customer relations and empower managers and staff. The result will be increased profits, enhanced competitiveness, and the self-confidence that comes from the ability to manage our destiny. In this way, we all win.

Introduction

This book can be read from cover to cover for a comprehensive understanding of computerized shipping systems or any chapter may be read independently.

Chapters 1 and 2 will help you understand what a computerized shipping system is and how it can benefit your organization in general terms.

Chapters 3 through 10 discuss specific features of computerized shipping systems. You will learn about the different communication methods that are typically utilized.

Chapter 11 is dedicated to customer service and the impact a computerized shipping system can have in this important area.

Chapters 12 through 15 discuss the various ways in which computerized shipping systems can be utilized to increase profit in a company.

Chapters 16 through 20 describe the choices that are available in acquiring a computerized shipping system and the questions you should ask in making a decision.

Chapter 21 is all about the implementation of a computerized shipping system and the steps that you can take to insure a smooth installation.

Chapters 22 and 23 are case studies that discuss how two businesses were changed by a computerized shipping system.

CHAPTER 1

What Is A Computerized Shipping System?

Over the past two decades, as computers have allowed us to do more things, more accurately and at greater speed, a subtle strategic and conceptual revolution has also taken place. Systems adapted initially to shave costs or improve efficiency, end up – if we give them half a chance – teaching us many things about our particular business and endowing us with new powers.

For example, most of us no longer keep manual general ledgers or hand type invoices and checks. First, with computerized accounting packages, we marveled at their speed and – if everything was input properly – increased accuracy. Now, push that program a little further. You will discover the ability to perform highly complex analyses about your business that would have taken hours or been impossible by longhand. Through

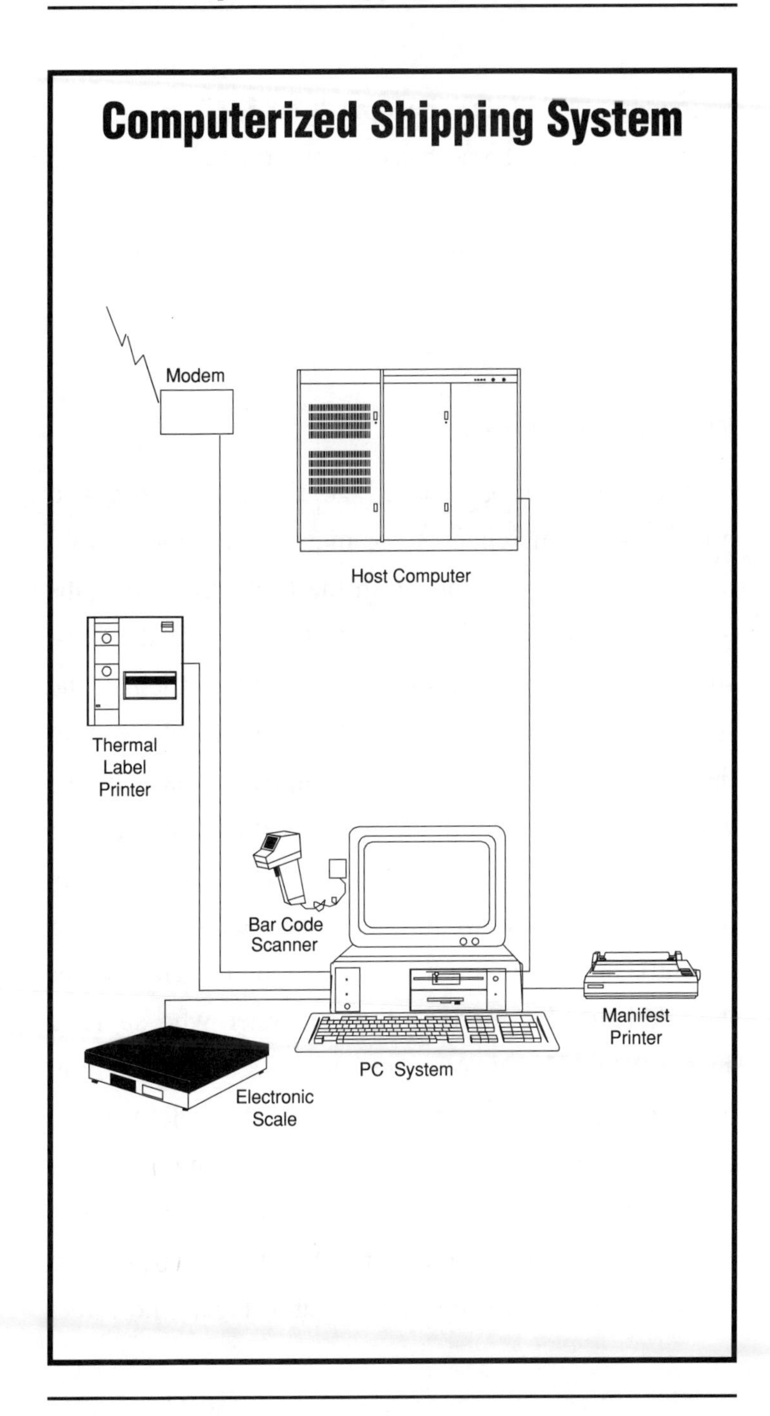
Computerized Shipping System
Modem
Host Computer
Thermal
Label
Printer
Bar Code
Scanner
Manifest
Printer
PC System
Electronic
Scale

computers, "What ifs?" become "Can dos."

As we review some basic shipping concepts, please keep in mind the "total package" of powers behind the software and hardware of today's modern business world.

What is Shipping?

Shipping can be defined as the preparation and processing of merchandise or material for transporting to a designated receiver. From the first camel caravans that crossed deserts to the first ships to sail the seas, shipping has always had the same basic challenge: the shipper must give his goods to the carrier for delivery to the receiver or consignee. The shipper gives a list of what is being shipped to the carrier, called a manifest or bill of lading. The fee for delivering the goods is usually determined by the weight, size, service level (air or ground), and destination of the shipment. The carrier then delivers the goods to the consignee who signs to accept them. This whole cycle, with its documentation, provides proof of shipment and proof of delivery to protect against negligence or loss by any of the parties involved.

It is not a simple job for any shipping department to compare rates, fill out forms and tags, and label packages, especially when there are 50 or more to be picked up on the same day. Imagine the time required filling out and maintaining the documentation for all those parcels. Errors and delays occur.

What is Computerized Shipping?

Computerized shipping is a process whereby a computer computes the charges, produces the carrier compliant labels, and communicates the results to the carriers, as well as your warehouse management system (WMS), accounting and customer service departments.

A basic computerized shipping system consists of a computer, interfaced to an electronic scale, label printer, and report printer. Sometimes additional printers are used to print airbills, Bills of Lading, or other documents. A modem is utilized for transmitting to and receiving data from the carrier. A bar code scanner can be utilized to input a work order number or package identification number. Today, most computerized shipping systems are interfaced to an organization's host computer, where the order entry or accounting system resides.

What Really Happens

In the case of a computerized shipping system, a transformation takes place similar to the one we discussed with accounting systems. It's so easy to tap a computer key and think we are just weighing a package or printing a label, as we did manually for so long. But an interfaced, computerized shipping system can serve as an "all-in-one" traffic manager, shipping clerk, and communicator with customer service and accounting. Among its powers, it can select the least expensive parcel carrier, generate appropriate carrier compliant bar code labels, and provide for instant invoicing. These systems can also reduce labor costs in shipping and accounting, improve customer satisfaction, and enable customer service to instantly respond to inquiries. All this can lead to improved cash flow and increased profits.

Perhaps even more importantly, managers and staff have more control of the shipping process and the power to integrate shipping into a total business strategy, on everything from inventory control and profit margins to staffing levels and customer service benchmarks.

Yes, we do start by holding a package in our hand. In the end, through understanding the power of computerized shipping systems, we can take our business to places we never thought possible. ◆

CHAPTER 2

Reengineering The Shipping Process

"America's business problem is that it is entering the twenty-first century with companies designed during the nineteenth century," write Dr. Michael Hammer and James Champy in their pioneering book, Reengineering the Corporation.

Imagine how antiquated the typical shipping department is! No wonder, this has been the last frontier to be computerized in many organizations. Even today, it is not unusual to find shipping departments manually routing and rating packages, handwriting shipping charges onto work order forms, and handwriting labels to be placed on boxes. Drawing on the insights of Hammer and Champy, and a real-world example, let's consider how the shipping process can be reengineered for productivity and profitability.

What is Reengineering Anyway?

"Reengineering is the fundamental rethinking and radical redesign of business processes to achieve dramatic improvements in critical, contemporary measures of performance, such as cost, quality, service and speed," according to Hammer and Champy.

The goal is not to make shipping departments better through incremental improvements – perhaps 10 percent faster here or 20 percent less expensive there. Instead, the reengineering paradigm, or process, seeks a quantum leap in performance – 100 percent or even tenfold improvements that follow from entirely new work processes and structures. The key is looking for those *broken processes,* or bottlenecks, that have the greatest impact on a company, both internally and externally.

Does your Shipping Department have Terminal Disease?

In looking for dysfunction in shipping, a common symptom of a broken process is the rekeying of data. I have commonly found that the shipping department, if a computer exists at all, is not connected to the company's business or accounting system. Consequently, the shipper will receive a report of the shipping charges and tracking numbers for each order, only to turn this report over to the accounting department to be keyed in for the invoicing and closing out of orders. Hammer and Champy pinpoint the problem; "If employees spend time typing in data from a computer printout into a computer terminal, whatever process they're working on is probably broken ... it is a symptom of what we call `terminal disease.'"

A Disturbing Example

In one recent project for a client, we found that the shipper had to enter 18 keystrokes in order to process a single package. The next day, an accounting clerk had to enter 46 keystrokes to update inventory, invoice the customer, and close the order. The clerk would bring up the order in the accounts receivable module of the company's computerized accounting system, and then enter the freight charges, tracking number, weight, carrier used, and date shipped.

Between the shipping and accounting clerks, there were 64 keystrokes for each of 50 orders a day. This totaled 3,200 keystrokes a day, 70,400 keystrokes a month, or 844,800 keystrokes a year! Keep in mind that this work was performed under pressure, with tight deadlines and frequent interruptions.

Extra work doesn't just consume more time and staff expense. This company's *broken process* led to errors that made for dissatisfied customers, as well as extra work for the customer service department.

Department of Defense studies show that the average error rate in recording data through manual key entry is 1 error in 300 entries. Using this ratio, the Key Error Rate for this company was 235 per month (70,400 keystrokes/300). Although it was difficult to measure the exact number of errors, as many undoubtedly went unnoticed, the customer service department was receiving several complaints a day of double shipments, wrong items, wrong quantity, wrong location, wrong shipping route (carrier service level), operator entry errors, invoicing errors from re-keying, or freight calculation errors. All these mistakes were attributable to the shipping department.

Research done at Texas A & M found that the average shipping error cost $50 to correct – on both the shipping and receiving ends. This does not take into account the added cost of damaged customer relations. A typical business often discovers that it is spending $30,000 or more to correct inaccurate shipments.

The Reengineered Shipping Process

When a business process or operation is reengineered:

- Several jobs are combined into one;

- The steps in the process are performed in natural order;
- Work is performed where it makes the most sense; and
- Creative technology is utilized.

In our example, we reengineered the client's shipping process by connecting the shipping department to the accounting system through the use of computer technology. This allowed the shipper to perform many of the tasks previously assigned to the accounting clerk. Now, the shipper simply scans the work order in the accounts receivable module. The shipper places the parcel on the scale, presses one key, and presto!, a bar-coded label comes out of the printer, matched to the carrier's specifications. The freight charges, tracking number, weight, carrier used, and date shipped are electronically entered, the order is confirmed, the inventory updated, and the invoice printed – *all in less than 20 seconds with a single keystroke.*

Reengineering the shipping process has enabled this client to achieve dramatic improvements in quality, service and speed. These improvements include:

- Elimination of errors;
- Elimination of customer complaints due to shipping errors;

- Customer service can provide instantaneous feedback as to the status of an order;
- A savings of 2 hours per day for the accounting clerk;
- Invoices going out the same day a package is shipped;
- Inventory updated in real time, providing more accurate stock levels for sales people;
- Better cash flow; and
- More orders can be shipped in the same amount of time.

For this company, computer technology has made possible a new, reengineered shipping process that is saving it thousands of dollars a year and increasing business and customer satisfaction through the elimination of a broken process.

A Final Note

Hammer and Champy ask, "How can we use technology to allow us to do things that we are not already doing? Reengineering, unlike automation, is about innovation. It is about exploiting the latest capabilities of technology to achieve entirely new goals. But applying information technology to business reengineering demands the ability to first recognize a powerful solution and then seek the problems it might solve, problems the company probably doesn't even know that it has."

Granted, this goes against the grain of conventional wisdom, which often suggests that we leave well enough alone. However, sometimes we simply cannot see the next horizon – and beautiful landscape – until we climb up to a new plateau. I invite you to take a look at your shipping process and ask: Is there an opportunity for reengineering? ◆

CHAPTER 3

Error-Free Shipping Labels

As carriers develop new services, they place ever-greater demands on shipping personnel to get the right label on the right package. Two, three, even four labels may have to be correctly placed before the shipment goes out the door.

Not surprisingly, this leads to confusion. United Parcel Service (UPS) mandates that the outside of a package include a return address, a ship-to address, and the shippers tracking number. These could be on three different labels. The shipper needs to add another label to track if it is Hazardous material. Similarly, FedEx with their FedEx Ground packages, has separate bar coded labels for their prepaid service, collect service, and air service.

Customer-Driven Label Requirements

Furthermore, many organizations are requiring shippers to place labels on packages to meet their own specific requirements. Kmart, Sears, Walmart, JC Penney, and B. Dalton all specify label formats. Other companies are following suit, specifying that the product code, UPC, purchase order number and other information must be provided, or they won't even *receive* a package.

In fact, many shipping companies are spending thousands of dollars for separate "label" computers that sit next to their computerized shipping system and produce both types of labels – the ones required by customers and the ones their own system uses when manifesting a package. This quickly becomes expensive. Above and beyond the initial cost of $10,000 - $15,000 for each system, a company has to pay for two labels, two maintenance contracts, and have their shipping clerk enter the same information twice!

So it is no wonder shippers are confused and shipping areas have dozens of different labels in piles, drawers, boxes, and rolls lying around. The process is becoming more and more time consuming and error prone. And the mistakes are not trivial. The difference between putting on a red label instead of a blue label can cost 100 percent more. Two labels that look very similar have different consequences; they determine who pays the freight!

Fortunately, some industries are starting to wake up to the confusion and costs of non-standard labeling formats. One of the tasks of the AIAG (Automotive Industry Action Group) — an organization on the cutting edge of EDI (Electronic Data Interchange) — has been to create standard label formats for the hundreds of different auto suppliers shipping to the OEMs (Original Equipment Manufacturers).

Computerized Shipping Systems to the Rescue

In the beginning, computerized shipping systems could automate rate charts and generate reports. Second generation systems had the capacity to print ship-to labels and COD tags. These older systems have become commodities; so much so that carriers like FedEx and UPS are actually giving them away. Today's more advanced computerized shipping systems interface with host computers in *real time,* utilizing customer-specific information to route the package and generate the exact label needed. The shipping clerk does not have to make decisions. He or she simply puts a package on the scale, scans or enters the package identification number, and pushes a button. The system produces a label that fulfills all carrier and customer requirements.

The computerized shipping system "sees" certain information about the order that enables it to eliminate human errors. It looks at the customer code or name, and follows an instruction that says whenever it "sees" Kmart, for example, it has to produce a Kmart label. The system also views the "ship via" code, adding to the label the required text, as well as the bar code that lets the shipper know to charge the consignee. Thus, in a fraction of a second, a computerized shipping system can follow specific instructions exactly, generating a single label with both *carrier* and *customer-driven* bar codes. The entire process is not only faster, more professional looking and error-free, but it can save companies thousands of dollars each year compared to existing manual systems. ◆

Airborne Express Shipping Label

FROM:
TAYLOR SYSTEMS ENGINEERING
40800 FIVE MILE ROAD
PLYMOUTH MI 48170
(734)420-7447

WEIGHT(LBS)
001

TO:

MARK TAYLOR
TAYLOR SYSTEMS ENGINEERING
40800 FIVE MILE ROAD
PLYMOUTH MI

REF# 11111

PIECES
1

ZIPCODE
48170

ORIGIN

SHIPMENT NO.
0000001002

SHIP DATE
02/12/2000

ADDITIONAL INFORMATION

PHONE: (734)420 – 7447

SERVICE DELIVERY DAY

EXP

SPECIAL HANDLING SERVICES

LIVW 5C
SBH

AIRBORNE
EXPRESS

0000001002

0.50 LBS

1 OF 1

From Pencil to Computer Chip

At one time, data collection in the shipping department meant writing in spiral notebooks and legal pads, or directly on work orders. Shipping personnel would record shipments by categories like department of origin, product classification, salesperson, customer name, and date and time shipped.

When computerized shipping systems were introduced, everyone was understandably excited about their reporting potential. Unfortunately, the standardized reports generated by these early systems were rarely useful. Producing nonstandard (customized) reports was a frustrating, time-wasting exercise, as information from several systems (e.g. shipping and billing) had to be "rekeyed" into a single format. Not only were such reports inordinately expensive to produce, but if managers needed information immediately for use in important decisions, they were out of luck.

Today's shipping systems can process inquiries and produce custom reports in any format desired. If you are shopping for a new computerized shipping system, or looking to upgrade your present one, and it does not have the capability of generating custom reports and graphs, you are looking at old technology.

As companies reorganize, merge, and become "lean and mean" to compete in a New World economy, near instantaneous access to information in flexible formats is paramount. Information in the shipping area can help managers evaluate the productivity of their staff, negotiate more competitive rates with their carriers, and provide comprehensive management analyses.

Who's the Boss?

Therefore, companies should be extremely skeptical about the "free" systems being offered today by major carriers. In most cases, these systems provide an *illusion* of convenience and savings, while severely limiting the information available to managers.

When this happens, it also limits management's power to negotiate rates and make decisions that impact an entire organization. Remember, a loss of information is the same thing as a loss of control.

Can Your System Do This?

Computerized shipping systems should be able to generate a variety of reports, including summary reports, exception reports and ad hoc reports. The system should also provide elementary arithmetic functions, such as calculating sums, counting, finding averages and finding the lowest and highest amounts.

Summary reports provide key data on the activities of the shipping department. An example of a summary report is a list of the total number of packages shipped for the week by job number, carrier, packer, shipper, salesperson, account, customer, and department.

Exception reports warn managers when results from a particular operation have exceeded or not met expected standards. An example of an exception report is a list of all the actual weights that exceeded the expected weights of the packages shipped. Another example is a list of the pickers whose productivity fell in the top or bottom ten percent of the organization.

Ad hoc reports are reports that managers need, usually quickly, to solve a specific, one-time problem. An example of this type of inquiry is a list of packages that were sent via air to, say, Zone 8. This would be useful for negotiating with express carriers. Another example is a list of all packages that were shipped after 5:00 PM. Such a report may help pinpoint an overtime problem. Overall, the ability to conduct customized inquiries about shipping operations eliminates the need to print out ream after ream of unnecessary (unread) standard reports. Instead, managers get speedy replies to meaningful inquiries.

The Big Picture

Often, the information provided by a shipping system is more easily viewed and understood as a chart, rather than columns and rows of printed numbers. An example of a useful graph is the number of packages processed for each hour of the workday. This can lead to more productive scheduling and staffing in the shipping room. For this reason, the best parcel processing systems also include graphics capabilities.

The Next Generation

Advances in parcel processing software are continuing to revolutionize shipping operations. In addition to being able to store more than one million shipping records in an historical archive database, these systems offer easier-to-use intuitive menus, protection against accidental corruption of data, easy-to-read screen displays, and "cut and paste" report formatting. The system can also export data files to a variety of other applications, such as Microsoft Excel or Access, Lotus 1-2-3, or word processors.

The Power to Manage

Usually, astute organizations quickly grasp the many qualitative aspects of a computerized shipping system.

These include:

Ability to examine more alternatives. With reliable information, it is possible to analyze alternative allocations of resources in a shipping operation and how these options would impact cash flow. Scenarios that would have taken days to construct and analyze can be viewed in minutes. For example, what would be the effect of changing the handling charge, or how much would be saved with an additional two percent carrier discount?

Ability to achieve a better understanding of the organization's shipping department. Being able to look back with intelligence makes it possible to look forward with confidence. Information can help managers identify trends, forecast future operations, and avoid potential problems.

Capability to provide information on a timely basis for control of ongoing operations. Information from a shipping system can provide a better picture of detailed cost by company, division and department. A report of packages shipped monthly can enable managers to spot deviations from prior months more quickly and take appropriate action.

Ability to achieve time and cost savings. It isn't hard to choose between a budget forecast that consumes 25 hours of a manager's time (spent sifting through stacks of papers, calculator in hand) versus one done in one-third the time with computerized reporting. The ability to perform "what if" types of analyses improves the quality of budget forecasts and other management planning tasks.

Capacity to make better decisions. Shipping information systems make it possible to consider issues and alternatives that otherwise may not have been explored. Increased depth and sophistication of analysis are possible. Access to this information gives managers the opportunity to make more informed – and verifiable – decisions.

The Bottom Line

We have seen that there is world of difference – and power – between the raw accumulation of data and the intelligent use of information. Through decisions based on information obtained from computerized shipping systems, management can cut costs, improve productivity and increase profits in any shipping operation. ◆

Sample Graph Via Computerized Shipping System

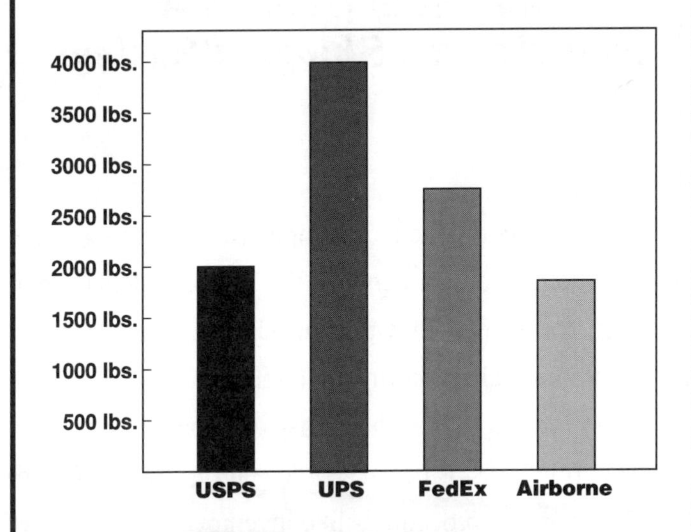

Weight Per Carrier

CHAPTER 5

Importing Data To A Computerized Shipping System

An essential component of computerized shipping is the ability to exchange data between the shipping department computer, sometimes known as an UPS manifest system, and a more centralized company computer, what is called the "host" computer. This host computer typically organizes (or "runs") a firm's order entry, invoicing and related accounting procedures like inventory.

There are several ways to exchange data between these computers – *import, export,* and *real time* – each with its own characteristics and advantages. In this chapter, we will discuss how data *import* has greatly improved the accuracy and speed – as well as overall productivity, professional image and profitability – of shipping operations.

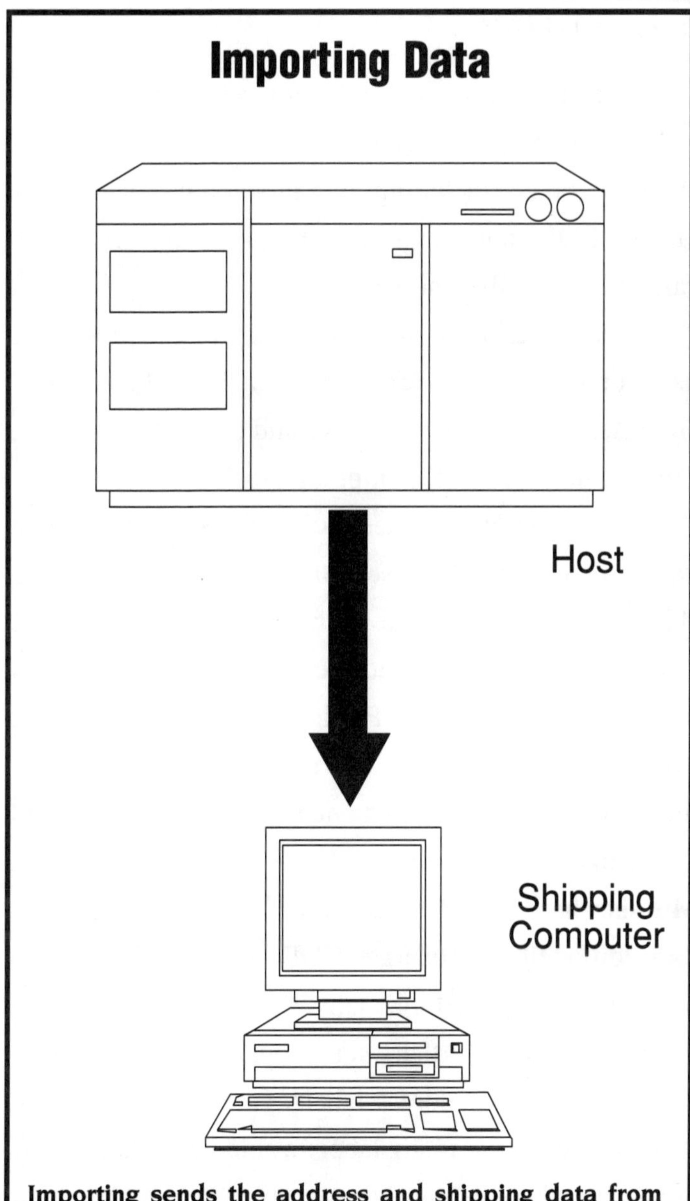

Importing sends the address and shipping data from the host computer to the shipping computer

Separate Lives

To begin with, the ability to import information into a shipping computer has led to the automation of many shipping tasks, including the preparation of address labels, COD tags, and airbills (used for overnight carriers like FedEx and Airborne).

A (non-interfaced) host computer might produce a hard copy invoice or packing list, which would be folded and inserted into a plastic sleeve and put on the package. This would serve as the shipping label.

As we know, with folded packing lists, it's not all that hard to accidentally insert the wrong address in a shipping window. We've probably all done the same type of thing once or twice (or more!) when paying a credit card or phone bill. Furthermore with this system, even if the address were positioned correctly on the box, the shipper would have to manually key the zip code and the package "ID" number to process the shipment. Mistakes here often lead to rating and billing errors.

Additionally, a separate COD tag or airbill would have to be completed manually.

Going a step further, some businesses use a *host computer* to print address labels. However, there is no way to predict how many labels would be needed, as the goods would not yet have been packed. It would be feast or famine, with the host computer printing too many labels, wasting money and paper (or not enough), which would mean writing a shipping label out by hand or a special trip to a photocopier to make extra copies of the packing list. Additionally, the *shipping computer* would still have to produce a *complimentary* label to meet the carrier's requirements.

Clearly, such a dual system is inefficient, costly, and invites errors compared to a single integrated label for every box that contains all the information needed for shipping. Through importing, only one "master" customer database (names, addresses and other information) need be maintained, which eliminates another potential source for errors.

Speed

With importing, shipping is not only completed more accurately, but also much faster. If the information from the host computer is complete, the shipper does not have to enter any data at all. If any item of information is missing, the shipper simply keys in the package identification number and fills in any missing information, whether package weight, carrier or type of service. The shipping computer then prints out the complete address label, COD tag, or airbill *in seconds.*

How It's Done

Convinced of the advantages of data importing, there are several ways we can transfer our "ship to" addresses from the host computer to the shipping computer, a process often referred to as *downloading*.

One of the simplest and least costly methods is to copy the "ship to" addresses onto a diskette, walk the diskette over to the shipping computer and import them manually. This method works well when the consignee (people that are shipped to) addresses do not change very often.

If the addresses are constantly changing or orders are being shipped the same day that they are received, then it becomes more efficient to link the two computers together. The best approach is to utilize *real time communication* (See chapter 7 for a further explanation), which allows the user to access the accounting or order entry program, subject to security restrictions, from the shipping department.

Putting It All Together

With today's computerized shipping systems, an *electronic file* containing all the addresses – plus known shipping data such as carrier, class or service type, and special services like COD amounts or Declared Value – can be sent electronically to the shipping computer.

The shipper need only put packages on the scale and type or scan in the package ID number; the shipping computer produces the labels, COD tags, and airbills in moments. In fact, if weight and other shipping information are already known, the shipping computer can automatically calculate zones and rates; produce complete shipping labels, COD tags, airbills; and manifest each package – without any operator intervention or keystrokes.

Faster, Cheaper, Better

In summary, through importing, your shipping computer will be able to generate all needed labels, shipping tags and airbills, doing away with hand writing or individual keystroking off of shipping documents. You speed up the shipping process, eliminate errors and reduce costs, while insuring that every package gets shipped to the correct destination. This leads to enhanced customer satisfaction – and profitability – for your shipping operation. ◆

CHAPTER 6

Exporting Data From A Computerized Shipping System

In the last chapter, we looked at importing as one way to exchange information between a shipping computer and a host computer. Next, we will examine exporting, where data is transmitted in the opposite direction – from a shipping computer to the host computer, where, for example, customer invoices would be generated.

As I often tell businesses, you can do it the hard way, or I can help you do it the easy way.

First, let's consider all the things that might need to be done or that can happen *after* a package is shipped.

Do you have to write down the shipping charges, date shipped, tracking number, picker, packer, and so forth on a shipping document? (By the way, how legible are these entries)?

Exporting Data

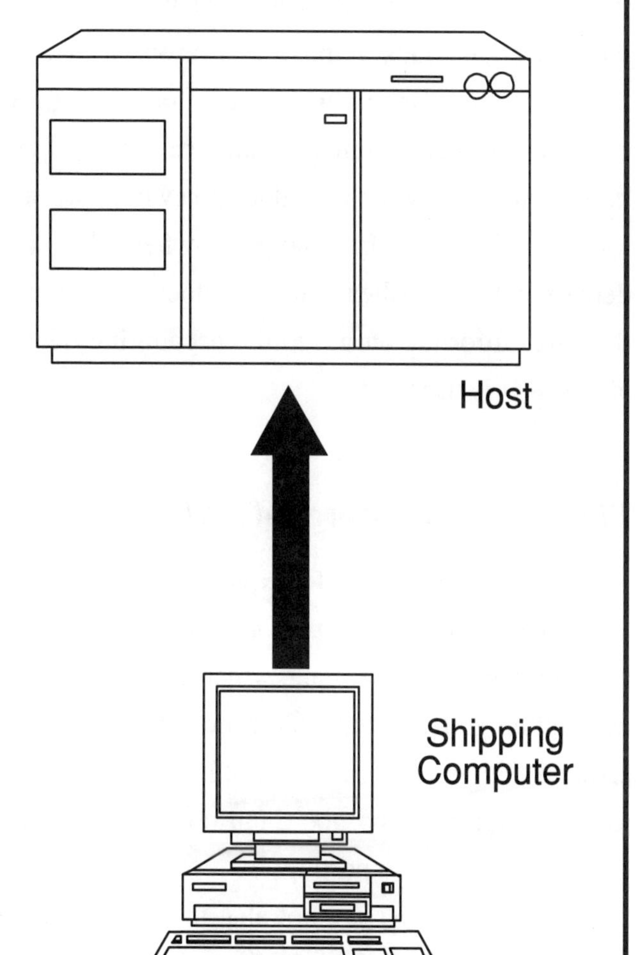

Exporting sends the shipping data, typically the freight charges and tracking information, from the shipping computer to the host computer.

Does your system print this information on a label that you then place on the packing slip? (By the way, do these labels ever get stuck in the printer or one with another)?

Maybe your shipping system prints information directly onto the document, which can also get jammed in the printer? (By the way, does this whole process take too long)? And what happens when the shipping department is finished with the documentation? How does this information get to the accounting department and how it is used?

The Easy – and Powerful – Way

Enough questions. Let's explore some answers.

At the first level, *exporting* eliminates the time it takes to manually enter data, which can save hours of an accounting staffer's valuable time, and also eliminates errors due to misinterpretation of handwriting.

That's all well and good, but now let's consider the strategic power of exporting.

Often, companies are not able to invoice for several days after shipping a parcel, because they are waiting to receive the exact freight charges from the shipping department. They may not get the data from shipping until the next business day, and it's even longer before the order can be "brought up" on the host system for manual entry of the shipping charges. With exporting, accurate data on even hundreds of packages can be processed in less than 10 minutes. This means that invoices can go out — and be paid — sooner, thus improving cash flow.

Next, exporting leads to (much) faster updating of inventory records. As we know, computerized shipping systems – by correlating product codes with quantities shipped – make possible today's *just in time* (JIT) inventory systems. Your customer service department also profits, as representatives are able to provide customers with reliable status reports of when an order shipped, the carrier utilized, and when it is expected to arrive.

Finally, electronic data export is helping make real the dream of a paperless office. Throw away that costly shipping room document printer and you also throw away paper and label jams, expensive ribbons and exorbitant service contracts. You no longer need file yellowing stacks of shipping documents. All the tracking information has been electronically transferred to the host computer.

Beam It Up

As we reviewed in the previous chapter, information can be transferred between computers by diskette, by a *local area network* (LAN), or by a direct link to the host computer. In this case, data exported from the shipping room computer to the host computer, called an *upload,* can include such items as carrier, freight charges, packer, tracking number, product, quantity, weight, and date and time shipped.

Exporting can be accomplished in a *batch,* where many records are pooled for entry at one time, or in real time, as each package is shipped. The latter method permits immediate invoicing, which can save postage expense if the invoice is placed in the package as it is being shipped.

In summary, the export of shipping data can increase productivity in both the shipping room and the data entry room, boost cash flow, improve customer satisfaction, and create strategic advantages that we will explore in much greater detail in the following chapters. ◆

CHAPTER 7

Real-Time Communication Offers Speed, Accuracy, and Powerful Use Of Information

In our hectic business world, it's often easy to confuse the "process" for the "principle." Computerized shipping systems should first be about managing information, not weighing packages. This information "stream" consists of many elements, including package weight, rates, carrier specifications, shipping labels, invoices and composite reports of shipping activity.

The common denominator in all this is information, or data. Thus, the computerized shipping system should really be the most accurate and productive way of managing data – on a transaction by transaction basis – through two-way live communication. Let me now outline the substantial advantages of such "on-line" systems.

Real-Time Communication

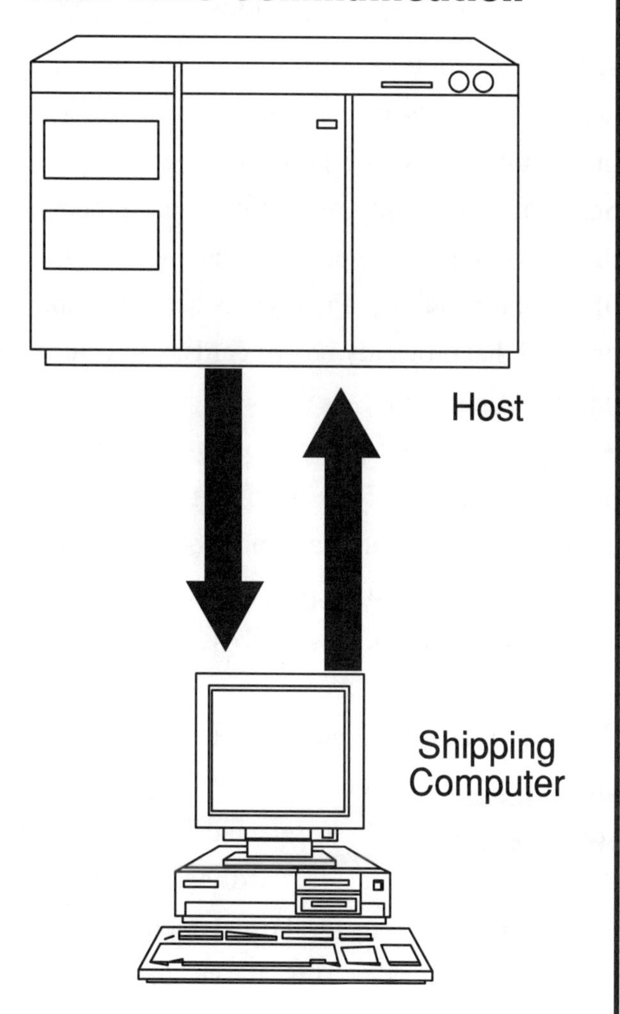

Real-time communication sends data between the host computer and the shipping computer on a transaction by transaction basis

Batch vs. On-Line Processing

The details of individual shipping transactions can be communicated to a host system (for integration and analysis) one-by-one in real time, as we will discuss more fully below, or grouped together in a "batch." Some of us probably remember batch processing from the early days of computers when the "batch" was a set of computer cards, all keypunched by hand. If you dropped that unwieldy box of cards, you could spend all day resorting them!

The main – and perhaps only – advantage of batch processing is that you need not be connected to a computer system at the time you are shipping. For example, you could ship 50 packages during the day and, at the end of the day, process all the transactions in a single group.

Batch processing, however, is extremely limited in power compared to on-line processing, (also called *live communications*). Here, selected information (such as the ship-to address) is read and then transmitted instantaneously from the host computer as a parcel is placed on the scale. This allows the host system to verify orders, complete and print invoices, print accurate packing lists, update inventory records, and record exact shipment times and tracking numbers – simultaneously.

The Many Advantages of On-Line Processing

Such systems are so embedded in today's culture that we often take them for granted. But each time we reserve or register for an airline ticket, rental car or hotel room, we are going "on-line." Imagine the headaches that would result if all these transactions were processed in a batch. Airplanes would likely never get off the ground.

For shippers, the advantages of on-line processing include:

The capacity to invoice customers at time of shipment.

As freight charges can be posted immediately after the package is processed, this system can be designed to "trigger" a printed invoice that is included in the package. This improves cash flow and saves postage: at just 50 packages a day, the savings in postage can exceed $300 a month.

The power of information feedback.

Data never becomes "stale." The batch system is inherently flawed, as the shipping computer is always working with an old database. If addresses are changed or new customers added, the batch that was sent to the shipment processing center is no longer accurate. Actually, on-line processing is more accurate *in both directions*. The host system is always working with and receiving correct information.

The ability to update orders almost instantaneously.

Consider a customer who orders a package to be shipped ground, but calls and switches at the last minute to next-day air. With stand-alone or batch shipping systems, someone must physically go to the distribution center and search through all the packages on the line. If you ship hundreds of packages or this occurs several times a day, this can be both time consuming and unproductive.

On-line processing eliminates this problem. You can bring up the order on the host system and change the shipping status without taking a step. The system will "read" this new instruction at the point the package is placed on the scale, and ship it by the correct mode.

Reduced processing errors.

Any chain is only as strong as its weakest link. Similarly, any data processing system ultimately depends on the "integrity" of individual pieces of information. Stand-alone systems with manual data entry are notoriously mistake prone. In fact, a Department of Defense study found an error rate of 1-in-300 with manual recording. This inaccuracy gets multiplied when freight charges have to be manually re-entered into the host system for the purpose of creating an invoice.

If you use a five-digit invoice number, the number of keystrokes required to process a single package and manually re-enter the freight charges would be 19. At 50 packages a day, this would be 950 keystrokes, or 20,900 per month. If we then divide this number by 300, we see that there would be 69 errors a month, even with the best operators. In contrast, an on-line system saves the time and money needed to "track down" and correct such errors.

More on the "Human Element"

When we discuss computer systems, it is easy to get "lost in the numbers" and forget the people advantages. Consider the airline and hotel reservation systems we discussed earlier. They not only help us to get from Point A to Point B faster and with greater certainty, but they also make possible a tremendous *dialogue* between company service personnel and consumers. On-line computerized shipping systems will save you time and money. They will also empower your shipping personnel to offer better service. Who really wants to walk back to the warehouse and look for that package that must be shipped next day instead of by ground? With an on-line real-time system, this becomes a breeze.

Overall, a live interface between your host computer and shipping system is far superior to stand alone manual systems or batch processing systems. It reduces labor costs and improves accuracy by eliminating time-consuming, error-prone manual data entry. With on-line transaction processing, you can invoice immediately, save postage, relieve inventory in real time, and update customer service people the moment a package is shipped. Finally, it provides shipping personnel with the most up-to-date addresses and carrier routing instructions, increasing quality and customer satisfaction. ◆

CHAPTER 8

Local Area Networks: Being "Connected" In The Shipping Room

Not too many years ago, in the heyday of pop psychology, if I were to use the word *connectivity,* we might think of getting in touch emotionally with others or ourselves. Today, the word has a new meaning, as we 'connect' with each other not only spiritually, but also electronically.

Individual computers in the business world are also increasingly being connected—or networked—to each other in what are termed LANs, for local area networks. This major innovation in computer technology has brought new speed to our business world. Each person, sitting at a single computer, possesses the logistical power of the entire system.

In particular, networking offers exciting new possibilities in small parcel shipping. Imagine typing

Network

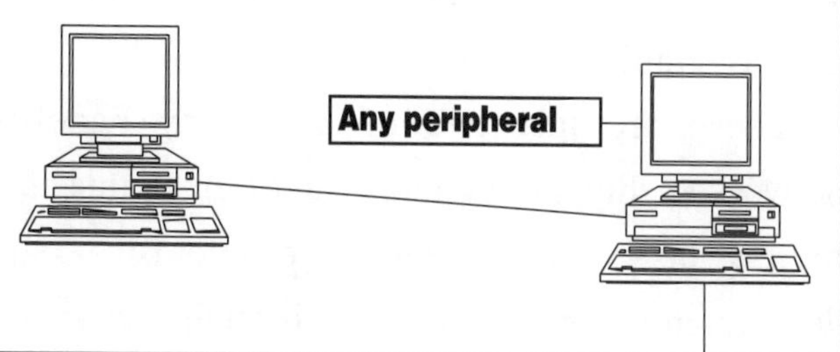

- All machines are processing simultaneously
- Each station can have a scale, label, printer, scanner, etc.
- All units are utilizing the same database and creating one history
- Searches, voids, reports, can be done from any station, any time

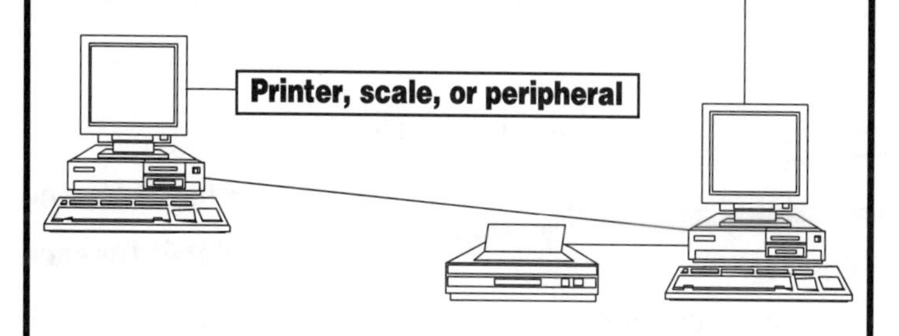

invoice numbers into a "front office" computer and finding out how and when the parcels were shipped—without having to walk back to the shipping department and interrupt operations. Or consider three or four shipping systems, each one integrated in real time to your billing and inventory departments, made to process parcels simultaneously.

These are just two of the many benefits that networked shipping systems can offer. In this chapter, I review how some common problems in shipping departments can be solved through networking of computers, as well as the different types of networks currently in use.

Some Typical Shipping Room Quandaries

Situation One: *Take a number, please!*

Picture a company whose parcel volume has increased to the point where employees are having to wait for each other to finish the last package before the next one can start. Other symptoms include: having a backlog of parcels when the carrier's driver arrives, escalating overtime costs, and never seeming to catch up. What do you do? One solution might be to just buy another computerized shipping system, but how would it access the database you are using to generate address labels and COD tags? And what if you have to trace a package; how will you know which system it was processed on? You will also end up paying for two daily pickups.

Situation Two: *Package 54, Where are you?*

Next, consider a company whose customer service department continually is bombarded with inquiries as to the status of shipments. Customer service representatives end up searching through reams of paper to find out how and when a package was shipped. If the answer cannot be found, someone has to walk back to the shipping department and disrupt operations while looking through the daily log.

Situation Three: *The Free Stooges.*

Some companies succumb to what I call the *multiple carrier syndrome,* where they allow several carriers to each provide "free" shipping computers and software. Consequently, costly confusion reigns. You are no longer able to comparison shop to find the least expensive route; customer names and addresses must be continually updated in a computer that someone else legally owns; and, should a customer call to locate his or her shipment, you must search through each computer system until you find the record.

To generate shipping activity reports, the information from all these systems must still be manually added together. If your firm charges freight and postage back to job numbers or department accounts, this will also have to be done manually. So much for automation!

The Solution

Networking of multiple shipping stations solves all of the problematic situations I have just described. Multiple workstations share a single database of customer names and addresses, and also produce an integrated manifest, eliminating the need for multiple carrier pick-ups. A single inquiry, void, or report can be generated from any terminal, even hundreds of feet away, as to the status of any parcel, from any carrier. A multi-user network also allows a shipper to charge back to departments or job numbers from any station, including those that interface with postage meters.

A networked shipping system is faster and less expensive than buying several stand-alone systems. There are both hardware and software savings. A networked system can share a printer and a computer hard drive (the network server), and multi-user software licenses typically cost less than the sum of individual licenses for each computer.

What You Must Know About Networks

Be sure you know what you need to get out of a multi-user computerized shipping system. A "true" network is a system that will allow any person to access any shipment history from any station on the network. Several companies claim their systems are networks, when, in fact, they offer workstations that will only merge data at the end of a day or when specified. In a true network, however, all users have equal access—in real time—to the same manifest, shipping history and consignee databases.

There are two basic approaches to the networking of computerized shipping systems. The first uses a standard network, like Microsoft's Windows NT or Novell. System Integrators or Value Added Resellers (VARs) may either sell just the shipping program (software), while the customer provides his own hardware, or a complete turnkey system. The advantage of this type of network is flexibility. You can install the system on an existing network, as well as update or change software without having to replace the "hard" parts of the system.

A second approach is to employ an integrated, proprietary system of software and hardware. This type of system can be designed exclusively for the shipping and mailing environment. Many such systems, for example, replace the standard QWERTY keyboard with a dedicated one. However, you will not be able to use other software programs on the same workstation.

As we have seen, networked shipping systems, in either case, are both quantitatively and qualitatively better than stand-alone, non-integrated systems. Save time; spend less; accomplish more. This is how we can all profit through technology. ◆

CHAPTER 9

"When Will It Be There?" You Ask

Finding The Best Shipping Route Through All The Fine Print

We all need timely, accurate and complete information to arrive at the most effective business decisions.

Imagine asking your travel agent the best way to get from Detroit to Jacksonville, Alabama as soon as possible (ASAP) and being given several choices of airlines and rates, but not the time that you would arrive? What would you do? How could you plan your day or make any commitments? One thing is certain, your business couldn't survive long – let alone succeed in a highly competitive arena – without better guidance.

Amazingly, many of America's best companies do something similar each day, shipping millions of packages without the information vital to achieving the most efficient use of resources or reaching benchmarks in customer service.

Some Problems

We are often in the position of Sergeant Joe (Jack Webb) Friday of the old "Dragnet" television series, who routinely deadpanned: "Just the facts." It's not so easy. It may be hard to believe, but whenever your company sends a package "Next Day Air," many, or most times you would guess wrong about time of arrival. Because of television advertising, you might assume that it would be there by 10:30 AM, and inform your customer so.

The fact is: No carrier guarantees that every package will be delivered by 10:30 AM. It's all there, in the very fine print of your airbill, which asks you to consult the carrier's delivery guide. There, you discover that delivery times can vary dramatically based on the specific zip codes being serviced.

Again, using the airlines reservation scenario as an example, how would you react if, after arriving in Jacksonville at 4:30 PM at a cost of, let's say, $1,550, you discover that you could have flown on a different airline and arrived four hours earlier, at 30 percent less cost. Wouldn't you be angry at your travel agent? This analogy holds true for shipping overnight packages.

The fact is: "Over 80 percent of customers who use parcel carrier services are misinformed of their options," according to the Official Express Management Guide (OEMG), the authoritative and independent guide developed by shipping expert, Sonny Smith.

If that isn't enough, now imagine finding out you had a third option to Jacksonville, where you would have arrived even earlier for only $800 – almost half of what you paid. If you were me, you would probably never do business with your travel agent again! Once more, the same thing happens over and over again with parcel shipping.

The fact is: "40 to 50 percent of the packages sent for Next Day delivery could be sent by a less costly means of transportation," according to the OEMG.

When traveling, you expect to be informed of all your options for routes, arrival times, and fares. Yet, every day, when you send parcels out the door, you don't have similar guidance. This leads, far too often, to upset customers; frustrated, "unempowered" personnel in the order entry, customer service and shipping departments; and excessive shipping expenses. Sonny Smith sums it up neatly when he concludes that "98 percent of customers make costly mistakes – daily."

What's Gone Wrong in the Express Industry

As you can see, your company may be wasting thousands and thousands of dollars each year on unnecessary shipping charges, all the while disappointing customers and staff alike.

While a deliberate campaign of misinformation may not be to blame, the fact is that all carriers that offer next day service actually have multiple delivery schedules. Some packages arrive by 10:30 AM, some at noon, others at 3:00 PM, and still others at 4:30 PM. Unfortunately, your shipping system may not be programmed with each carrier's delivery service guide.

As a result, you may very well choose a priority service – at a premium of as much as $15.50, thinking your package will arrive at its intended destination by 10:30 AM, when the carrier has *made no promise* to deliver it before 4:30 PM. Worse yet, a competing carrier likely has a discounted afternoon service that would get the package there at the same time, perhaps at half the cost. Remember our airline example?

Overall, most package carriers are reliable, or they wouldn't remain in business. Yet, they often don't take the time to fully explain all possible shipping options, as it's not in their financial interest. In fact, if you sign up on an exclusive basis with a carrier to get one of their "free" shipping systems, you have no way of comparing.

It's like calling only one airline, instead of using a *good* travel agent.

Sonny Smith says that, "The U.S. Postal Service has lost a 9 percent market niche in the express services area, not because it's their fault, but because the manufacturers of computerized shipping systems and scales let the customer choose express service to zip codes that they don't even service. When the package doesn't arrive when expected, the post office has been blamed."

Many carriers are paid millions of dollars for premium services they *haven't even promised* to provide, because they realize that most shippers don't read the small print in the service guides. Some carriers don't even give you one of their guides unless you ask for it. Let's face it, even if you wanted to, comparing rates and delivery times between several carriers on multiple packages is an overwhelming task.

The Solution

Don't throw in the towel, convinced that shipping costs must be "rolled into" your overhead, or passed along to customers. The astute ones don't accept this way of doing business. The others shouldn't.

The solution is a computerized shipping system, programmed to handle all that fine print in each carrier's delivery guide. It quickly, easily and cost-effectively provides your company with the data needed to make intelligent shipping decisions.

With a computerized, real-time interfaced shipping system, your order entry or shipping department is also able to *immediately* answer customer's inquiries on how an order will ship, how much it will cost, and the transit time. An order entry person can select the most appropriate way to satisfy a customer's shipping requirements at the time the order is placed, or a shipping clerk can determine the best way at the time of shipping.

With all the facts at our command, it is clear that a computerized shipping system allows us to make the right shipping decision each time – saving money, sparing employees and winning customers. ◆

Delivery Profile Screen

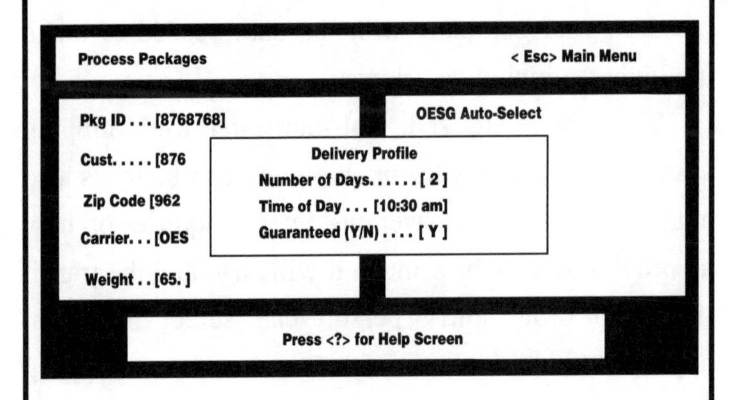

Carriers Matching Delivery Profile Menu

Carriers Matching Delivery Profile

CARDESC	CHARGE	TIME EST	TIME GUAR
CARRIER A	$ 16. 75	10: 30	10: 30
CARRIER B	$ 17. 50	3: 00	3: 00
CARRIER C	$ 24. 25	10: 30	10: 30
CARRIER D	$ 25. 00	10: 30	12: 00

CHAPTER 10

Expert Shipping Systems

Even an apparently simple package shipping assignment can soon involve a rather complicated *decision tree* if our goal is to *always* find the best rate and route. Factors include such things as ground vs. next or second day air and promised delivery times; service levels of different carriers; and rates of different carriers, including negotiated discounts. Also, as long as we're filling out a shipping wish list, let's add calculation of COD and insurance charges; labels customized for each carrier we use and each company we ship to; and real time interfacing to our accounting and inventory systems!

No doubt HAL, the computer in Stanley Kubrick's *2001: A Space Odyssey* would feel insulted if given such an easy task, but a computerized expert shipping system employs a similar form of Artificial Intelligence (AI) to help us make quick, accurate, cost-effective shipping decisions — almost as soon as the package hits the scale.

Furthermore, intelligent shipping systems provide expert knowledge that allows managers to control the shipping process, eliminating – if that is what we want – the need for shipping associates to make decisions on the line.

How An Expert Shipping System Works

An expert shipping system "decides" by working through a series of algorithms, what might be called "rules of thumb." These rules are derived from high-level expertise gained from top experts in the shipping field, then augmented with the experience and specific needs of a company's shipping and traffic management team.

These algorithms typically consist of a series of "if/then" *conditional* statements, an example being "If the package is a COD, *then* a handling charge is added." However, most shipping decisions involve more than merely applying a single rule. In the COD example just given, other related conditional statements may apply, such as, "Should it be regular COD or certified check only?" or, "Don't add an additional charge to any orders going to our branch offices."

More complicated situations are addressed through a series of "multi-if/then" statements, such as: "*If* the package is COD, *then* add an additional $3 to the handling charge, unless it is being sent to a branch " or, "*If* it is a specific type of customer, *then* place the statement 'certified check only' on the COD tag."

In a further example, let's say that a certain ground carrier is able to fulfill all of your requirements – except for delivery to a certain area of the country. The expert shipping system could be designed to use that carrier for all ground packages, except for Zone 8, or except for a certain zip code (or even except for a specific customer). This could be accomplished automatically, or the operator could be allowed to override the decision by choosing from a set of options at different stages of the shipping procedure.

It isn't getting any easier. We need expert shipping systems to keep pace with the ever more complex services offered by carriers. For example, a carrier introduces a new three-day service. When should it be used? An expert shipping system can be programmed to handle such a complex decision as: "*If* the parcel is going to Zone 5 or above, *then* use the three-day service, unless it is a Zone 2, then use a local delivery service."

Where Are The Savings?

Researchers at Texas A&M University found that up to 2 percent of received shipments are in error, at an average cost of $50 to correct. *A typical company shipping 100 packages a day could find itself spending as much as $30,000 annually to correct errors made on the shipping line. In contrast, you can expect to save 10-15 percent in freight costs (regardless of your error rate) by using an intelligent shipping system.*

An expert shipping system can eliminate errors in several ways. First, procedures are followed exactly. Second, the system can check for human errors and display appropriate error messages. For example, an expert shipping system can check the actual weight of a package to see if it is out of tolerance with the expected weight, thus halting an improper shipment. An example of this might be when more of an item is packed than was ordered.

Additionally, the *knowledge* and *experience* with which your expert shipping system is endowed can transcend time and space. The same programming can be used in multiple sites or applications, simply by duplicating the necessary hardware and software. Once completed, expert shipping systems also preserve, or *codify,* the valuable expertise of experienced shippers who may retire or leave the organization.

Finally, an expert shipping system may cost less than maintaining (well-compensated) experts on staff, particularly in situations where similar types of analyses are repeated from month to month or even year to year.

The Final Voyage:

The Hidden Powers of Expert Shipping Systems

Far too often, in all areas of our lives, we make decisions based on impulse, or incomplete knowledge. In the business world, such uninformed decisions can cost us not just dollars and cents, but customer satisfaction and employee confidence and loyalty.

By combining the knowledge of shipping experts with the experience of shipping managers, expert-shipping systems can serve as reliable "stand-ins" that represent and protect the policies of management. We can decide things both *faster* — and *better,* avoiding those regrettable, spur-of-the-moment decisions made by individuals under stress.

Furthermore, shipping data can be consolidated and analyzed, allowing objective evaluation of the decision structure. Were we right in using Carrier A for all overnight deliveries? Or does it really make sense to ship by "ground only" west of the Mississippi? At any time, the logic and objectives *inherent* in the expert shipping system can be easily adjusted, to better serve new management priorities.

In summary, expert shipping systems provide many benefits for shipping departments. Used intelligently, they can eliminate shipping and billing errors, reduce freight costs, and empower management. ◆

CHAPTER 11

Leveraging Your Shipping Operation For Superior Customer Service – And Profits

In today's intense business world, often only price and customer service can set us apart from the competition. Gaining an advantage requires the interest and ability to look at each aspect of a business anew, seeing where it might be improved.

As Michael Hammer, author of Reengineering the Corporation, writes, "Applying information technology to business reengineering demands the ability to first recognize a powerful solution and then seek the problems it might solve, problems the company probably doesn't even know that it has."

One of these powerful technologies is a computerized shipping system, interfaced in real-time to your general business and accounting system. Such systems can significantly reduce shipping costs, while dramatically improving customer satisfaction. The net result will be a smoother running operation – and enhanced profitability.

Let's look at some typical customer service scenarios and see how an interfaced, computerized shipping system can turn challenges into successes. Have you encountered any of these situations before?

"No News is Bad News."

One of the most common problems encountered by companies in the order entry and customer service area has historically been an inability to access shipping information at a moment's notice. A typical call – whether innocent or irate – from a customer asking when an order was shipped can set off a frustrating, time wasting, chain of events.

It goes something like this. First, the Customer Service Representative (CSR) takes the customer's request, with a promise to call back as soon as possible. The representative then has to either interrupt the shipping department or search manually through reams of paperwork to find the required information. This may include such details as the date the order was shipped, the carrier, the class of service, and the carrier's tracking number. For C.O.D.'s, add the amount the carrier is supposed to collect.

Now, perhaps 30 to 45 minutes later, this representative, having stopped everything to get this information, begins a costly game of "telephone tag" to reach the client. Employee time is wasted, phone bills soar and your customer wonders why it took so long to get the answer to what seems like a very simple question.

In contrast, imagine if your customer service representative could simply type a few keystrokes and give the required information directly to the client. The difference is a computerized shipping system interfaced in real-time to your accounting system. Such systems can immediately provide your customer service department with "any and all data" regarding a package, the moment it is shipped.

"I've Changed My Mind."

Another common service challenge occurs when a customer calls back with revised shipping instructions. A ground order may be changed to next day air, or the delivery address may need to be corrected.

If the order has already been processed, and the work order is in the shipping department, your customer service representative must (again) walk back to the shipping department, interrupt operations, and find the order to change it. Worse yet, maybe the package has already been shipped. Recently, one of our clients told me that they were spending an average of 30 minutes per event, 10 to 15 times a day, searching for the right package.

Compare this waste of time and energy to what can be accomplished with a computerized shipping system, which can be easily integrated with your order entry system. The customer service representative knows in seconds whether the package has already been shipped. If it hasn't, any customer elections can also be changed in seconds. When the shipping system is integrated into the order entry system, the carrier, mode of shipment and address – in addition to billing or invoicing – can be changed up to the second the shipper places the package on the scale.

"What's the Best Way to Have this Shipped?"

This was once a much, much simpler question. For example, in 1980, there were only two major small package carriers: the United States Postal Service and United Parcel Service (UPS). Now, not only are customers much more knowledgeable and particular about how a product is shipped, but there are simply so many more choices, as well as conditions to meet. I call this C4 – the Constantly Changing Complex Carrier syndrome.

While competition generally favors customers, as you can see, finding the best and least expensive way to ship an individual package can easily become a bewildering task. "In fact, more than 70 percent of shippers overpay anywhere from 20 percent to 80 percent by not comparing services and rates," according to the 1992 Official Express Management Guide, published by Express Management Services of Atlanta, Georgia.

Again, a computerized shipping system leads us out of this world of confusion. Following the parameters given by your customer, it can be programmed to select the least expensive carrier. One of our clients (who ships 100 packages per day) reported, "This program alone will provide us with an annual savings of $18,102."

"I *Want it Shipped* MY WAY."

One of the greatest advantages of a computerized shipping system – if the reasons listed previously aren't enough – is that it can be easily integrated with new technology. A great example is the ubiquitous bar code, found on nearly every item in our neighborhood grocery or drug store.

Now, major retailers such as Kmart and WalMart and automobile manufacturers are among the many firms demanding that products be shipped with specific bar code information affixed. This is the "first line" of today's sophisticated inventory management and distribution systems. Companies often refuse to accept packages without bar coding, or, at the least, refuse to pay for freight costs. By assigning a "flag" to each customer account, integrated computerized shipping systems can distinguish specific customer requirements and produce the appropriate bar code labels.

The Common Denominator

In summary, today's customers are demanding more from your shipping department. This may include requests for labels with "proprietary" information; shipping packages on the day ordered; the selecting of specified carriers and service modes and, of course, instantaneous tracking information.

An interfaced computerized shipping system can meet all of these demands. In addition, it will be capable of being adapted to the shipping challenges of tomorrow, as both the competitive environment and your business evolves. This is the real power of technology.

Everything else being equal, if your company is able to respond better than the competition to customer needs, you will gain market share. With a computerized shipping system, your shipping department can be transformed from a cost center into a customer satisfaction – and profit – center. ◆

IT'S NOT EASY: SOME FACTORS TO CONSIDER WHEN SHIPPING PACKAGES

Carrier Selection

Today, we have tremendous choice in carriers, especially as the carriers expand their operations, domestically and internationally.

Airborne	FedEx
BAX Global	Local or Regional Carriers
DHL	UPS
Emery	US Postal Service

Service Distinctions

It's not enough to select a carrier. Each has rules and regulations regarding such items as:

Residential vs Commercial	Next Day A.M. Delivery
Dimensional Weight	Next Day P.M. Delivery
Insured/Declared Value	Second Day Delivery
Hazardous Material	Third Day Delivery
Delivery Confirmations	Letters versus Packages
Saturday Delivery	C.O.D. Delivery
Same Day Delivery	Package Tracking
Early A.M. Delivery	Pre-paid or Third Party Payment

The "Total Package"

The alert company representative must understand such issues as:

Time Sensitivity
Shipping Costs & Values
Package Weight
Package Size
Customer Credit Status
Carrier Accessibility
Type of Material
Traceability
Residence versus Business Addresses
Shipping Distances and Zip Codes

CHAPTER 12

Making Your Shipping Department A Profit Center Rather Than A Cost Center

While the sales staff of any business typically provides the first, and most lasting impression on customers, the shipping department is a close second. A poor operation can undo all your hard efforts; an efficient one can secure customers for life.

Since the cost of freight is typically passed on to customers, managers often look at shipping as a fixed cost. However, the average shipping operation, handling perhaps as few as 50 packages a day, can realistically achieve savings of 15 to 20 percent through improved systems and technology. The shipping department now becomes a profit center, with savings in time and money that translate into business leverage.

These are observations, based on working with more than 10,000 companies of all sizes over the last twenty-five years.

The first area of opportunity – rate shopping – is one that has barely been explored by companies until quite recently. Let's take a scenario I see quite often, where 50 packages a day or less are shipped:

- A sole vendor is used for each category of package: overnight; packages weighing less than 100 pounds; and heavier packages.

- The company pays list price for ground shipments and overnight service.

- Ground packages cost $3 - $5 each, air parcels $11 - $15 each. The weekly freight bill averages $1,000.

- The sales department or front office *instructs* the shipping department as to which carrier to use for a given package. The shipping decisions are *not* made in the shipping department.

- The package is sealed, weighed and shipped. The freight charges are routed back to the front office – *another paperwork step* – to be added to the invoice.

Sound familiar? Through rate shopping, this mythical company could save at least 15 percent on freight costs – about $600 each month. Here's how it's done.

Interstate Ground Shipping.

Let's start with ground packages. If you have more than ten out-of-state packages a day, you should be able to negotiate a discount – starting around 8 percent – with your carrier. Otherwise, shop around.

In some cases, it may pay to join forces with other small businesses. There are several business cooperatives that have hired professionals that negotiate substantial discounts for its members. These organizations deduct their commission, usually about 30 percent from the savings. A good cooperative will stay on top of competitive prices and shipping trends, constantly working for the maximum discount possible.

Intrastate Ground Shipping.

If most of your shipping is within a particular state, the savings can be even greater. In most states, there are local carriers that deliver within large metropolitan areas or regions. Again, if you average ten packages a day, you can command savings of 15 to 20 percent.

Overnight or Air Shipping.

Here, the urgency of the situation sometimes clouds good business sense. Never pay list price for air shipping. Even if you have only two or three air shipments a week, you may qualify for discounts of up to 30 percent. Sometimes, this is accomplished by settling on one carrier for all your air shipments, front office and back, or, as stated previously, by joining a cooperative.

Professional Consultants.

Another strategy for obtaining better rates is to hire a professional transportation consultant on your own. They will usually conduct a complete analysis of your present costs, volumes, and weights as well as negotiate the discounts, and audit your bills. Typically, they consist of former managers from the carriers and possess the inside knowledge and benchmarks of the discounts that you deserve. This gives them the power and knowledge to obtain savings of 30% or more for their clients.

Computerized Shipping Systems.

Now that you have a strategy, you need a cost-effective system for implementation. Computerized shipping systems can streamline the process of matching zip code, weight and urgency levels to a specific carrier, as well as actually filling out and processing the appropriate paperwork. Beware of carriers that offer "free" computerized shipping systems. You will relinquish your negotiating position, flexibility and control.

A *System that* Pays *for* Itself.

Even for smaller companies, the cost of an automated shipping system will be amply returned in continued savings on shipping. In some cases, you may choose to bill your customers the customary list price for shipping, which directly increases the bottom line. Depending on the marketplace, you may choose instead to pass the savings on to customers, which can improve your pricing position relative to competitors.

The next three chapters will detail specific ways you can turn your shipping department from a cost center into a profit center. ◆

CHAPTER 13

Save 40 Percent On Delivery Costs

One of the implications of information technology is the ability to create new classes, or distinctions, of service. We are all familiar with this principle through the telephone companies, which have ushered in everything from call waiting and call forwarding to universal, "wherever you go" telephone numbers. Special rates have also been developed for specific calling patterns and frequency of usage, whether it's a certain time of day, area code, or individual numbers.

The shipping industry is embracing new technology in a similar fashion. For example, your company could save thousands of dollars each year by utilizing services being offered by UPS and

FedEx Ground. The services – *Hundredweight* from United Parcel Service and *Multiweight* from FedEx – can earn your company 20 to 40 percent discounts off standard ground rates. Both rely on the information power of today's computerized shipping systems.

The "Deal"

Any shipper sending multiple packages to the same destination can qualify for significant discounts either through UPS or FedEx Ground if:

- Packages are addressed to a single consignee at one location;
- No single package exceeds 150 pounds, or 130 inches in length plus girth; and
- Total weight is at least 200 pounds for ground shipments, or 100 pounds for air shipments (UPS only).

Past a particular minimum weight, the consolidated shipment price will be less than the accumulated per package prices.

The Problem

Sounds great, but setting yourself up for these discount programs takes some pre-planning.

As it now stands, many companies do not take advantage of services like Hundredweight or Multiweight because they can't be sure that the *total* weight of shipments for the day will meet the minimum requirements. Or, they may have customers that place several orders throughout the day and unless a customer service or order entry department is paying very close attention, the company can easily overlook consolidation opportunities.

Similarly, those in the shipping department have no way of anticipating possible consolidations. It is simply too time consuming and too tedious to stop the regular shipping flow to hold back shipments for staging, which can then mean re-labeling boxes, voiding them in the manifest and reprocessing them.

The Possibilities

The good news is that computerized shipping systems can process shipments as single orders throughout the day, then later sort through the entire day's shipments and "optimize" them to take advantage of consolidated shipment discounts.

For example, such systems "see" that there are more than 200 pounds (for ground shipments) going to a single consignee, take those packages off the ground manifest, and automatically move them to the Hundredweight manifest to realize a discount. You needn't void packages or make manual entries in a manifest book. The system does everything automatically.

Also, since computerized shipping systems can print the necessary bar-coded shipping labels and assign tracking numbers, boxes don't have to be re-labeled.

The Profit

The exact discounts for Hundredweight or Multiweight are negotiated carrier by carrier, based on such factors as freight class, quantity shipped, total weight and the carrier's own profit margin. Remember, you can save as much as 40 percent on a single shipment of 200 pounds to Zone 8. With air shipments, the savings are even more dramatic. Those shippers sending multiple boxes to the same customers can save thousands of dollars each year by using services like Hundredweight and Multiweight.

95 percent of shippers employ *pre-pay* and *add* policies for billing freight charges back to their

customers. Thus, the majority of shippers are able to continue billing for the standard shipping charge, and keep for themselves any discount they are able to negotiate. This difference is a real dollar savings that more than offsets the investment in computerized shipping technology. Or, depending on productivity in other areas of a business, all or some of these savings can be "passed on" to customers, improving your competitive posture. ◆

Savings Through Package Consolidation

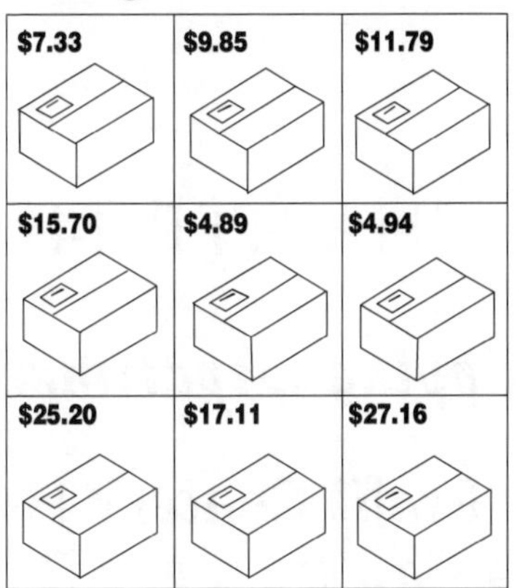

Total shipping charges for 9 cartons shipped individually: $123.93

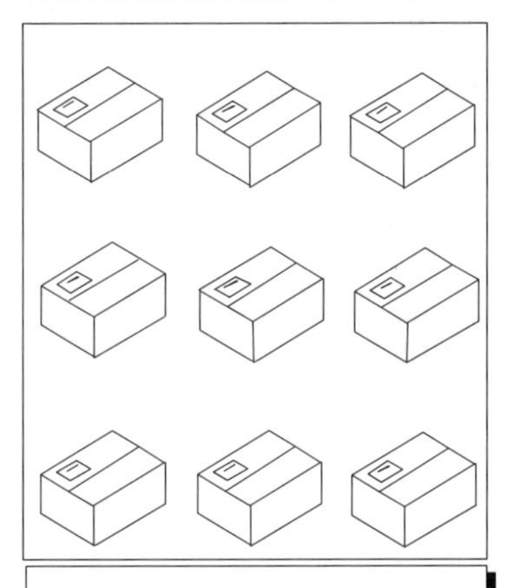

Consolidated rate for 9 carton shipment shipped hundred weight: $78.64

36% Net Savings
$45.29

CHAPTER 14

Shipping Department:

Cost Or Profit Center? Handling Charges Can Increase Revenues

Most companies view shipping departments as overhead expense — just another cost of doing business, like raw materials, rent, or salaries. It needn't be so. This chapter will describe how many businesses today are using shipping and handling charges – along with the increased efficiencies of a computerized, interfaced shipping system – to turn a traditional cost center into one that generates meaningful profits.

What is a Handling Charge?

A handling charge is an extra amount of money, billed to the consignee or customer, which you add to your actual freight expense. We are all familiar with the late night TV shows that advertise some new gadget or music CD and then remind us to add $4.95 for shipping and handling. Another familiar example is the Sunday newspaper supplement ads that always have a line item (typically filled in as a customer convenience!) for shipping and handling.

In the past, many manufacturers and distributors hesitated to add a handling fee, fearing customer reaction. Of course, in those days, almost everyone shipped UPS and there was only one price sheet. Back then, shipping systems consisted of a register that put a tape with the charges on the box, making it more difficult to charge the recipient a different freight amount.

A New Way of Looking at Things

In the mid-80s, as many new carriers and computerized shipping systems entered the shipping scene, we saw an increase in the number of organizations charging a handling fee. Today, just about every company charges something. Some people have asked me, is this legal? Is it justified? Is it ethical? My answer to all of these questions is yes. Let me explain.

Today, almost every shipper pays a different amount for freight. In fact, alert companies shop between carriers such as UPS, FedEx and Airborne, often negotiating discounts of 10-30 percent. Such discounts, in turn, help justify investments in integrated computerized shipping systems that can effectively determine the least expensive carrier.

There is nothing illegal or incorrect in charging customers the standard rate and keeping the discount. This is similar to a manufacturing company that invests in a new processing machine that saves costs. Depending on the competitive environment, some of the savings might be used to adjust prices, the rest go toward yet more investments or making the company more profitable.

Is it justified?

This follows from what we have just discussed. If the investment in a computerized shipping system costs a company an extra 50 cents per package, isn't it appropriate to add this fee to the cost of freight and handling? It is very common for organizations to charge a handling fee as a means of justifying investments in automation. Since computerized shipping systems do not put the charges on the shipping label, end users need not know your carrier's actual shipping charge.

Is it ethical?

I generally ask people that pose this question if they inform their customers how much they pay in materials, labor or fixed costs for the product they sell. As you might expect, they usually don't. Similarly, why should it be thought unethical to mark up freight costs to help pay the cost of shipping packages?

Shipping a package is more complex than it may seem at first. There are many costs involved, including the box, the cushioning material, the labor to package and label the parcel, the equipment used, maintaining storage space, and so forth. Companies like Mailboxes Etc. actually make part of their business one of marking up freight costs. For all companies, these costs can be tracked and calculated on a "per package" basis, to arrive at an average handling charge to be added to orders.

Sometimes You Feel Like It; Sometimes You Don't

Many companies charge only some of their customers a handling fee. Examples where free shipping is provided include backorders, large orders or special incentives by the sales department. To accommodate these situations, computerized shipping systems can be programmed to add or not add a handling charge based on parameters such as company name, total invoice value or a special code. This is especially true of shipping systems that are integrated into the order entry or accounting system, not the limited, "free" systems offered by many carriers.

The New Flexibility

Today's computerized shipping systems that interface with a company's accounting program offer rich strategic options when it comes to charging for shipping.

For example, some companies charge only COD's (which are more work) or certain accounts based on "customized" standards, such as the value of the total order. Other companies charge a flat dollar amount, like $1.00 per package, or charge on a per order basis. Still others charge a flat percentage of either the freight total or the invoice amount. Yet other companies charge the customer the regular UPS fee and keep the difference from whatever discount they can negotiate.

We had one client ask us to program their system to charge one rate for customers west of the Mississippi and a different rate for those east of the Mississippi. Many charge based on the size of the order. The more the customer orders, the lower the charge, and, at a certain level, no freight is charged. Another client had us set up their system to charge a different amount based on the size of the box used to ship the goods. If you are planning to buy a computerized shipping system, make sure it has the flexibility to handle the wide range of shipping schematics you are likely to use.

Overall, most businesses today add handling charges to shipped orders. They are legal, ethical, fair, and an excellent way to justify the investment in a computerized shipping system. Consider a customary freight bill of $5 - $7,000 per month. Even a modest 10 percent handling fee will generate substantial income for new investments that, in turn, increase business efficiency and profits. ◆

CHAPTER 15

Alternative Insurance Programs: An Important Marker On the Low-Cost Shipping Road

When it comes to shipping, some companies are still stuck on the high-cost road. They may use outdated, inefficient manual shipping procedures; have no sound way to track the status or location of a package; fail to negotiate among carriers for the best rates and service; even waste thousands of dollar each year insuring parcels with the carriers.

On the last count, be advised. Carriers such as UPS or FedEx are not going to inform you of insurance alternatives, since insurance premiums generate significant profits for them. To be sure, your money is better spent on more efficient shipping systems – or enhancing your own bottom line! Let's take a closer look at alternatives to carrier insurance, an important step on what I'd like to call the low-cost shipping road.

The Present System: Paying through the Nose!

If a package valued in excess of $100 is lost or damaged during shipping, someone must make up the loss, unless the shipper has purchased insurance. In most cases, that insurance is purchased from the company that ships the package. Like flight insurance at airports, this is the most expensive insurance for the coverage received.

United Parcel Service (UPS) builds $100 of insurance per package into the basic rates. Beyond that, a shipper must declare the value of the package and pay $0.35 for every $100, or portion thereof, over the $100. (Air carriers like FedEx and Airborne charge even more!) As an example, a package worth $750, would have 6.5 units of declared value. Rounded up to 7 units and multiplied by $.35, this makes for an additional fee of $2.45 (7 x $.35).

For this fee, if the carrier loses or damages the package, the insurer could be reimbursed for the full value of the parcel – but only after submitting a claim, including proper proof of value, and a sometimes lengthy investigation. Where's Columbo when we need him!

If the company shipping the package does not declare value, the most the carrier is obligated to pay is $100.

How Would You Like to Pay Up to 60 Percent Less?

I am frequently asked how a reputable, A+ rated insurance company could offer parcel insurance for as much as 60 percent less than the carriers.

I think the main reason is that the carriers charge a standard price for insurance, regardless of who is shipping the package. This means that my Aunt Shirley, likely an inexperienced shipper who doesn't really know how to properly package goods, and whose risk of damage is thus significantly higher, pays the same rate for insurance as a company that ships regularly and has substantially fewer claims. Like the automobile insurance discounts given to good drivers, good shippers can obtain significant discounts on their parcel insurance.

How Does it Work?

Alternative insurance companies provide coverage for lost, stolen or damaged parcels that is equivalent to the carriers. If a claim should arise, it is first submitted to the carrier. After the carrier pays the first $100 of the loss, the shipper sends proof of the claim payment to the alternative insurance carrier and receives payment for the balance of the insured value. Also, the whole process moves faster, because carriers usually don't take as long investigating these smaller claims.

Most alternative insurers charge a monthly premium, based on a report of shipments. Not only do you get to keep your money longer (most carriers bill weekly), but the reports are less tedious than the ones required by the carriers. If you have a computerized shipping system, the report can be created with the simple push of a few keys.

Who Cares, the Customer Pays the Shipping Cost Anyway!

Most companies ship their goods pre-pay and add, which includes freight charges. When using alternative insurance, many shippers are able to still charge the customer the carrier's rate – and legitimately pocket the difference. This is no different than if you were able to reduce your company's truck fleet insurance or other fixed costs by a certain percentage.

Depending on the competitive environment and long-term business strategy, these savings can help reduce the price you charge customers, be invested in new technology and systems, or applied to your overall profit margin.

The choice is yours, since most customers will be unaware that you are saving money in this way. If you choose to pass the savings on to customers, then at least, market the fact that you are doing so. Otherwise, charge what the carrier charges, bill your customers accordingly, and set aside the extra money to fund your own insurance program.

We Never Have Any Claims. Why Bother Insuring?

Technically, if your terms are FOB factory, the goods "belong" to the customer once they leave your building. By insuring packages, you are essentially taking on an additional responsibility, one that clearly enhances your reputation for customer service.

You may have been fortunate enough to not yet lose a package. Yet, one of the major carriers admits to losing or damaging 10,000 packages every shipping day. Thus, it is only a matter of time before a carrier loses or damages one of your packages. Competitively, if you don't insure, the customer might begin to question your other business practices.

The Complete Package: Computerized Shipping Systems Increase Savings and Efficiency

If your company invests in a computerized shipping system, you can earn even lower premiums, as much as one-fourth less, because insurance companies understand that such systems provide better tracking and accountability.

An interfaced, computerized shipping system can be programmed to automatically calculate the insurance fee based on the value of the package and then add this fee to the invoices – without a single keystroke by an operator. You profit from an error-free shipping system, where no one can forget to insure a high-value package.

How Much Can My Business Save?

If you insure on a daily basis, the savings can be significant. For example, if you insure just 20 packages a day for $500 each, you would spend over $7,000 a year in insurance costs. Through an alternative insurance company, you could save as much as $4,000 each year. To qualify, your company must spend about $1,000 annually for parcel insurance.

In summary, insuring your parcels with a carrier is like throwing money into a bottomless pit. When you come back, everything is gone. Instead, with alternative insurance companies, you can achieve outstanding customer service standards, while maximizing cash flow. That's a road I like to travel. ◆

CHAPTER 16

Beware Of Carriers Bearing Free Gifts!

In today's cost-cutting environment, every business is looking for ways to reduce expenses. Many times, what appears as an opportunity to save money actually ends up costing the company profits. More and more, small parcel carriers like United Parcel Service and FedEx, are offering their customers "free" computerized shipping systems with which they can process their parcels.

Thousands of shipping managers across the United States are accepting these systems with intentions of doing their own company a favor. On the surface, it appears to be a great offer with an opportunity to save money. Is there a catch? You bet. This chapter details 19 reasons why you and the management of your company should carefully consider the implications of accepting a carrier's "free" gift.

What haven't the carriers told you?

1. Free Choice

If you were presented with a choice between the carrier's "free" system or a discounted shipping rate, which would you choose? Of course, they may not present you with such a choice, or they may already be offering a discount and the "free" system. The reality, however, is that they would much rather give you a system.

As a manager of one of the major carriers recently told me, "We would prefer to give away a system rather than an additional discount because the systems have a limited cost and discounts are forever." Often, the carrier builds the cost of the computer, the software technology, support staff and service into their rates. Considering these built-in costs, giving away a system is actually more profitable for them.

Most shipping managers who accept the "free" system simply do not see what they could do with a discount. I have heard the following reasoning, "We pass the freight on to our customers anyway; so who cares if we get a discount? A "free" system saves us money because we don't have to make lease payments or buy a computer."

Unfortunately, these shipping managers are not taking into consideration the possibility of not passing on the discount, but rather the regular freight charges to their customers, which is the standard practice. After all, if you ship enough to receive a quantity discount based on your volume, why should you give it away? If you have other economies of scale from quantity purchases, do you give those away just because you bought right?

An additional 1 or 2 percent savings on your annual freight bill could amount to thousands of dollars in profit. These savings would more than offset the cost of a computerized shipping system provided by an independent third party, who has your best interests in mind.

2. *Rate Shopping*

When you accept a "free" carrier system, you are not only giving up a discount with that carrier, but you are giving up the possibility of shopping for the most economical rate for the service used. A shipper with as few as 50 packages a day can save 10 to 20 percent on ground shipments and up to 50 percent on air shipments through rate shopping. This "free gift" probably would not have the competitor's rates on it. Even if it did, it could be programmed such that the carrier could manipulate service selection to protect their own profits.

The carrier is "giving" you their system so that you use only that carrier. *That* is the hook! In comparison, a gas station could offer you a free car, with the stipulation that you must buy gas from them for the life of the car at the price they designate.

3. *Service Shopping*

Carriers offer many different services such as priority, third day, and select delivery. They use their jargon, and their systems are structured so that the operator chooses a service based on that jargon. The consequence is that an operator can pick a service that is misleading or in fact, wrong. They may choose priority service (at a premium price) thinking that it will be delivered the next day by 10:30 AM, when in fact, the carrier does not even offer that guaranteed delivery schedule. Carrier supplied systems do not pick the most economical service because it is not in their best interest. But then again, that is why they give you the system for "free."

On the other hand, multi-carrier shipping systems provided by independent suppliers offer the capacity to shop for a service based on need or urgency level. They offer choices based on delivery time, day of the week and cost. They are often designed to use the language that your company uses and provide the choices that are in your best interest. The savings generated can be significant. For example, the difference between a next day letter that is guaranteed to arrive by noon and one that is guaranteed to arrive by 5:00 PM can be as much as $10!

4. Multiple Package Discounts

A company that ships multiple packages to the same destination can qualify for discounts of up to 40 percent. The carrier offers these discounts because they are delivering them to the same address. Importantly, their "free" systems may not automatically consolidate packages and apply discounts.

Independently provided multi-carrier systems, on the other hand, can actually tabulate the number of packages that were shipped at higher individual package rates that day. If certain requirements are met, they automatically change the billing classification and apply the discount. The potential savings are phenomenal.

5. Higher Insurance Rates

The "free" systems utilize the declared value or insurance rates provided by the carrier. The advanced tracking and accounting capabilities of vendor supplied systems, on the other hand, can result in a 50 percent savings in insurance costs. If your packages are worth over $100, these savings will pay for a system on volumes as low as 20 packages shipped a day. Of course, carriers, like the car rental companies, would rather have you use their insurance because it is more profitable for them.

6. *Zone Skipping*

Sometimes, it is financially beneficial for you to send your packages by truck across a couple of zones, and then drop them off at a carrier's distribution center. This capability is not available in carrier supplied "free" systems because it undermines their revenue objectives. An independent, vendor supplied system is specifically designed to meet your revenue objectives and can provide manifests to another zone, which can result in significant savings.

7. *Integration*

Most carrier-supplied systems don't integrate on a real time basis with other PC-based systems or host system applications. This limitation prevents the shipping system from becoming an integral part of a company's total information environment. A vendor-supplied system can integrate with the customer service application and provide second-by-second information on the status and tracking of parcels as they are shipped, improving customer service response times.

8. *Invoice Automation*

Another negative aspect of using a carrier-supplied system is the cost of invoicing the customer *after* the package has been sent. The loss realized can be substantial when you consider the cost of data entry, data entry errors, postage, and labor costs associated with obtaining overdue payments. Vendor systems that integrate with your business accounting application or host system and can produce an invoice at time of shipment, eliminate these costs and reduce turnaround time, providing for increased cash flow.

9. *Query/Reporting*

Most carrier-supplied systems provide standardized reports. Multi-carrier systems, however, may provide a *report writer* from which the shipper can design and customize virtually any type of report. This allows the shipper to combine carrier information and analyze it in a way that is unique to his or her business.

10. *Carrier Performance Auditing*

Vendor supplied systems offer carrier performance monitoring capabilities. If a package is not delivered by the guaranteed date or guaranteed delivery time, the system has an auditing function that will report on this information and the amount of the refund due.

Less than 10 percent of shippers claim refunds when a carrier does not fulfill its guaranteed delivery time. This potential savings is not taken advantage of with the "free" carrier system . Rarely do carriers point out these potential savings. A good multi-carrier system offers this important function and can save shippers hundreds and sometimes thousands of dollars a year.

Often, carriers do not want to share their performance information with their customers, and therefore, will not offer any auditing features. This represents another lost opportunity for those using a carrier-supplied system.

11. *Multiple Applications*

Today, many vendor-supplied systems can provide applications beyond shipping such as receiving, labeling, mail processing and more. These applications can integrate a company's entire information environment and provide benefits for the entire company. Such technical functionality is not within the capabilities of the carrier-supplied systems. Companies with these technical requirements should look at the multitude of benefits a vendor system can provide.

12. *System Service/Maintenance*

The technical aspects of any shipping system require timely and responsive service. Because vendor supplied systems are backed by companies whose main objective is to service their systems, they have more resources and are in a better position to respond directly to customer needs. Carriers are not in the computer business. Typically, they do not have adequate technical staff in the field to service customers effectively. In fact, many carriers must hire a third party, who is not always entirely familiar with the software, to service their systems. Don't rely too much on the information you are collecting on these systems – or rather, the information the carrier is collecting on you.

13. *Adaptability*

In general, carrier supplied systems are not particularly designed to adapt to the shipper's unique processing environment. These systems are geared toward the carrier's business environment and billing practices rather than the shipper's. Carrier-supplied systems help the carrier streamline data entry procedures in *its* accounting department.

14. *Expandability*

New features and enhancements to your shipping system cannot be easily implemented with a "free," carrier-supplied system. Vendors of multi-carrier systems have the resources and are structured to make ongoing system enhancements to meet the needs of its clients. The vendor's primary focus is on systems development and meeting *your* information needs.

15. Cost of Marriage

If you are utilizing a "free" system, you are indeed, married to the carrier who supplied it. Remember the analogy of the "free" automobile. You must use their gas for the life of the car.

Once you have said, "I do", you become a captive audience. You do what the carrier wants. You have been given a system with no monetary investment and are not in a strong position to demand anything. The carrier now has a distinct advantage. Don't look a gift horse in the mouth, right?

There are a few questions you should ask yourself about the "free" shipping system. What happens to your company if the carrier who supplied that system goes on strike? What is the cost of not being able to ship for several days or even weeks? What will the CEO of your company say about the decision to accept a "free" system then? *It might be time for a divorce.*

16. Fox in the Chicken Coop Syndrome

Once you accept a "free" system, you relinquish some control over your business and information about your business. The carrier supplied system is oriented towards *their* interests, *their* profits, and *their* way of doing business, not yours. It is like letting the IRS do your tax return. The carrier will always be working toward achieving their own financial and logistical goals, more often than not, at your expense.

17. Proprietary/Confidential Information

Years ago, computerized shipping systems simply printed out labels and a report at the end of the day. That's what carrier supplied systems do. Today, shippers realize that these systems also store a wealth of information, much of it confidential, about the identity of customers, products, departmental budgets, and invoice amounts. Do you want this information in the hands of a third party who may have regular contact with your competitors?

18. Negotiation Leverage

Although carrier supplied systems are "free" of upfront charges, the actual cost of the system is factored into any future discount negotiations. If a customer challenges the discount program, the carrier will often threaten to remove the system. Greater discounts more than offset the cost of a multi-carrier system that provides greater functionality and productivity.

If you are working with a particular carrier try the following strategy:

First, beat the carrier down on price, *then* ask for a free system. Next, ask the carrier to keep the system and deduct the $50 a day they estimate the "free" system is costing them. This sounds like you are actually doing them a favor.

19. *Competitive* Edge

History shows that competition is good. It promotes technological advances and innovation in any industry, including ours. The constant threat of competition keeps carriers on edge. It forces them to strive to be the best in service, price, and convenience. If the threat of competition is removed, carriers become lackadaisical and less responsive.

Not long ago, there was very little competition in this industry. At that time, the major carriers typically treated customers unprofessionally and offered few service options. I prefer to keep the carriers on their toes, forcing them to maintain the type of quality service we all deserve.

The threat of removing systems if volumes are not high enough or if other carriers are considered is one of the tactics used by carriers to manipulate customers into becoming dependent on their services. It is easy to be taken advantage of in this manner and to become blind to the hidden costs associated with carrier supplied systems.

Conclusion

Although a carrier system can provide basic shipping functions, its technical limitations and associated hidden costs make it a less than desirable option for many companies. A full-service, independently provided vendor supplied system can provide advanced functionality, integration and additional cost savings in the long run. Vendors represent *your* interests.

Carefully consider the above points before making this important *business decision.* ◆

CHAPTER 17

Let The Buyer Beware: How to Purchase An Interfaced Shipping System

Remember the difference between the snake oil salespersons in the days of the Old West and today's salespersons of "do it all" shipping software? The snake oil hawkers *knew* when they were lying – when their product couldn't deliver on its promises. Similarly, in the past several years, more and more companies are claiming that they can interface their shipping system with a client's existing accounting or business system. Unfortunately, many sales representatives may be sincere in their promises, but they are sorely lacking in their understanding of shipping system technology.

As a consumer, your company assumes the risks and consequences. Wasted management time and MIS resources or lost freight savings may be just the tip of the iceberg. Some faulty installations have led to expensive and time consuming law suits. In the past two years, we have replaced dozens of systems – many of them less than a year old – which, clients maintained, 'never worked.' The old adage, "Let the Buyer Beware" applies. The best strategy to prevent a costly mistake is to thoroughly research the vendors you are considering.

The following five steps should be taken when choosing a vendor:

1. *Assemble a Project Team.*

An interfaced shipping system benefits the whole organization. It is critical to get the right players involved, so they can provide input as to their needs and concerns. Shipping management will want to make sure the system handles processing for any freight carrier. Your MIS department or computer consultant will want to know the level of programming and support required. Accounting will need to specify how invoices will be updated with freight charges and what procedures will be used for backorders. Customer service will want to know how the system can improve response time and tracking information. Additionally, a senior manager or executive should be on the team to spearhead the project through intra-company politics and bureaucracy.

2. The Safety Net: Get it in Writing.

Draft written specifications of what you expect the system to accomplish and then have the vendor sign off, promising to fulfill the requirements by a designated time. Include all carriers and services that are to be utilized, sample label layouts, and sample report layouts. Specify exactly how you want the interface to work. If you have any special requirements for handling charges or COD's, spell them out. The next two chapters will give you some ideas of what you should include in your requirements specification. When the vendor's salesperson says, "No problem," put it in writing.

3. Seeing is Believing.

Observe the system in action, interfaced into the platform you are using. If you are on a Novell network, ask for a demonstration on another client's Novell network. Don't be fooled by a company's size or national presence. (Pretend you're from Missouri and tell the vendor, "Show Me.")

4. Deal with Experience.

Check a minimum of three references of companies (preferably ones close enough to visit) that have purchased systems interfaced into comparable platforms. When you reach the operations manager, ask the following:

- How long has the system been installed?
- What host computer and software are they using?
- How many packages do they ship per day?
- Is the system interfaced on a live, real time basis?
- Have they experienced any problems?
- How quickly and how well has the vendor responded to problems? Is *local* support available?
- Most importantly, would they do business with this vendor again?

Far too many buyers don't bother calling references. That is a major mistake. You don't want to be the guinea pig. Your objective is to research several companies that have circumstances and applications similar to your own.

5. *Deal with Competence.*

Determine the qualifications of the installation team. Are they engineers or technicians? Do they have college degrees in engineering? Are they A+ certified? Do they have Microsoft certification? Are the salespeople merely looking for an order, or are they professional consultants that can help you design a system and justify its cost savings to your entire organization?

Overall, your organization or business can generally realize tremendous savings and productivity gains with an interfaced shipping system. The advantages include: the ability to shop for the best carrier and best rate for each package; error free, real time invoicing updates, which makes it easier to "pass on" shipping costs; and improved productivity, as accounting personnel no longer have to physically check a shipping log or hunt to find out if a package really was shipped.

Choose wisely. ◆

CHAPTER 18

How to Select the Right Shipping System For YOUR Organization

Choices. Choices. Choices.

This is what makes the American and global economies so rich and powerful. It also means we must do our homework, no matter what level of consumer we are. While this chapter might seem like it has more questions than answers, it was done on purpose. I want to highlight that the choices you make about your computerized shipping system, and it's customization, are critical to increasing your productivity, reducing your operating costs, and boosting the morale of your employees. The wrong choices can be costly, time consuming and frustrating.

Thus, the intention of this chapter is provide you with concrete examples of what you should look for in your shipping system; how to make sure that you get what you expect. And nothing is fixed in stone; you must be alert to new carrier requirements or products, new capabilities, even new shipping regulations or "standards of service." As technology and the services provided by carriers change, so also will these criteria. Please check our website, **www.shippingsys.com,** from time to time, where we will post updates to the material in this chapter. As for all those important questions? Here we go:

Who is complaining, your shippers, customers, your boss or everyone? What problems are you having with your present shipping system? Where's the "ouch" factor? Where have bottlenecks or complaints come from: frustrated employees who just hate having to ship something (Does your key operator position keep turning over?); carriers who keep issuing you warnings or penalties; or angry customers? Next, as much as possible, quantify the issues in terms of both time and cost. This analysis is important for overall strategic business planning (How much do we spend on shipping and what savings are possible?), as well as for actually justifying the new purchase or upgrade of a computerized shipping system.

The major rationales, or needs, for replacing a shipping system usual fall under the following: elimination of mistakes; need to increase capacity or combine processes, such as shipping with billing or shipping with inventory; overall quest for cost savings or better productivity; and compliance with new carrier and/or customer requirements.

Typically, a company's shipping volume has increased and the old system is not able to grow; or it is opening a new distribution center. Sometimes, managers or operators are fed up with system snafus or difficulty in use; or see the many benefits of integrating multiple business systems. Unfortunately, companies often realize the benefits of replacing a carrier-provided "free" system when it's too late. Even in the shipping room, empowerment applies.

What carriers should be included? Next, decide which carriers to include in your shipping system. Some considerations include:

- Do we include the U.S. majors, such as USPS, UPS and FedEx?
- What about specialty carriers like Airborne, DHL, Emery, and BAX Global?
- Local or regional carriers and couriers?
- Less than truckload (LTL)?

- Do you have your own company trucks that should be a part of your system?

Overall, there are many cost control, audit and customer service advantages to having every package that goes out the door recorded in your shipping system. Additionally, if the system is adjusting inventory records, creating ship-complete postings, or triggering an invoice, it might make sense to have every package shipped go through the system, including customer pick-ups and deliveries by salespeople.

Projected usage. Now that you have determined what carriers you would ideally like in your shipping system, you need to determine what quantity of shipping you do with each of the carriers. Let me explain why getting back to basics is important. While it might sound nice to have all the carriers you ever would possibly use on your system, it might not be cost-justified, because most of the time the cost of a shipping system is increased with each carrier added. Also, some carriers, like FedEx, have specific volume requirements in order to qualify for its most advanced automation services. And, such add-ons can cost as much as $3,000 to $5,000 per carrier.

The ethical computerized shipping system vendor

will explain this when quoting a system. He or she should also review the three basic levels of processing parcels.

A. **Record-keeping only.** You simply record the fact that you shipped a package with a specific carrier. This record will include the carrier name, time and date shipped, and may allow you to enter a tracking number or pro number and print a label. This process is ideally suited for recording customer pickups and your own deliveries. It is often used for keeping track of LTL shipments.

B. **Processing by carrier's rates.** The advantage of this method is that the freight charges are recorded. Now, you can invoice customers for freight and reconcile bills from the carrier. This method usually will produce a label, or a bill of lading if it is a LTL shipment. With small package carriers like Airborne, it may involve completion of a pre-printed airbill. This is an improvement over a manual system, but less expensive than processes that require the purchase of the carrier's "full compliant" module. I would recommend this level of system for infrequently used carriers or when package volume is less than 10 per day with that carrier.

C. **The carrier's compliant module.** This

method creates a carrier-specified thermal label (See the examples in chapter 3). The label's bar code will incorporate special routing information that helps automate delivery. Rates and routes are updated automatically by the carrier or your vendor. At the end of the day, the operator transmits an electronic file to the carrier of all packages shipped. This is used by the carrier to generate your bill for services, as well as to start the location tracking process on the carrier's web site. This state-of-the-art (for now) approach is the way to go if you ship 20 or more packages a day with a specific carrier.

Fine-tuning carrier service. Now, we choose among many carrier options, including:

- Domestic and international services.
- Hazardous materials.
- If you ship with the USPS, do you need to integrate with a postage meter, or, with an electronic postage system, such as E-Stamp?
- Do you ship hundredweight?

Overall, never assume that a certain functionality comes with a given system. Ask your vendor a lot of questions.

Much more to think about.

Management of charges. Will you need multiple account numbers with a carrier? Your company might ship packages on behalf of another company; do you want a specific account number for that company? Or would you like different divisions within your company to have their own account numbers? Some organizations want to charge every shipment to a specific department code. Shipping systems can be set up to verify that the right code is entered, even matching ongoing expenses against that department's budget or allowance.

What if you pass on freight charges to your customers? Some considerations include:

- Do you need to keep track of both the retail rate you charge your customer, as well as the discount rate you pay? Or vice versa, are you passing savings on to your customer but want to let them know how much you have saved them?
- For example, some companies ship packages by air, but only charge ground rates in order to compete with a local company on price and delivery.
- You may want to charge a different (discounted) rate for backorders or when a mistake was made on an order, as a customer service tool.

- What about handling charges? If employed, will these be a flat dollar fee or a fixed percentage of the freight cost? Does it apply to everyone, and if not, what are the exceptions? Some companies charge fees according to box sizes, others determine how much by the dollar size of the order. Decide on a company policy in advance of implementation.
- Will you ship cash due on delivery (COD); if so, will CODs be limited to a single package or be on every package in the order? For example, in order to avoid having a customer accept all the packages except the one with the COD attached, some companies make sure every package is shipped COD. But charging for every box sent out by your company will increase freight charges quite a bit. Maybe you will want to do it both ways.

Keeping track with customers. Have you been bombarded in the past by inquiries about the details of shipped packages? One solution is to have the computerized shipping system automatically send an email or fax to your customers the moment the package is shipped. You can tell them how many packages, tracking numbers, COD amounts, and when to expect delivery. What about the following?

- Have you been billed back from carriers for address corrections? Your shipping system can be configured to verify the consignee's address with a third-party database, which reduces costs and shipping delays.
- Multiple invoices in a single box can be hard to track down later, unless you request a system function called "SWOG" or "Shipped With Other Goods." SWOG generates a separate record for each invoice shipped within the box, helping confirm or close out orders with your interfaced accounting system.
- Order accuracy. Have you been shipping the wrong item or wrong quantity of an item? Do you need to know exactly what is in each box, including such details as serial numbers, for Electronic Data Information (EDI) purposes? This is accomplished through pack verification, a feature which prompts your shipping room operator to scan a barcode on each item as it is packed. In real time, the system will verify that the correct quantity is being packed by checking against your business system's original order record.

Standing in line? Would you like the ability to prepare packages ahead of the time you intend to ship as Internet and web-based commerce develops. Just think about all those collector's plates or Elvis dolls that are waiting to be shipped during the holidays. In some cases, companies, such as video production companies, can only ship packages on release dates. Since they may be shipping thousands of packages at a time, they like to process them through the shipping system, put the bar code labels on the boxes, and hold them until the release date. We call this "pack and hold" or "future ship."

Or how about shipping from multiple zip codes; what is termed drop shipping, or zone skipping? Say you have a large volume of small packages that need to be shipped a great distance. They can be made ready for shipment in one site, then trucked to a carrier's distribution center elsewhere. You can save many zones of freight charges and save considerable expense, even with the trucking cost figured in.

Security. The Internet age and computer hackers have made us exquisitely sensitive to this issue. Remember, not only are your business records often integrated with your computerized shipping system (especially if you taking advantage of its full powers), but you hold in trust information about your vendors and customers. Expect to hear more and more about this as electronic commerce continues its burgeoning growth.

■ Who should have access to the setup and

configuration utilities of the shipping system? Will passwords be used? Will certain functions be "controlled"? For example, will an operator be able to void packages on their own, or will supervisor approval be required?

- How many users will the system handle at any one time? Would you like to have the ability to determine carrier rates and assign tracking numbers at every customer service person's desk? This allows all service people, not just the ones physically shipping packages, to better serve customers.

Rate Shopping.

As the comedian Billy Crystal says, don't get me started, for rate shopping is one of my favorite topics. For good reason. Choosing among carriers and their unwieldy maze of services, is one of the most complex tasks your system will be called upon to do. Think airline schedules and rates. We are close to that level of complexity. And these rates and conditions are not static, but constantly changing, just like the airfare from Baltimore to St. Louis. The stakes are high, for this is where you can realize great savings.

Moreover, it may sound obvious, but when it comes

Moreover, it may sound obvious, but when it comes to setting up your shipping system, you must be sure that it is configured to shop using the discounted rates that you have already negotiated from your carrier. Why? Most shipping systems come programmed with the carrier's retail rates. But if you can justify a computerized shipping system in your organization, it also means that you have enough volume to qualify for discounted rates.

These discounts vary, depending on the carrier, for different service levels, weights, and zones. In other words, you could have a 15 percent discount for ground packages up to 20 pounds; and a 20 percent discount for packages from 21 pounds to 150 pounds. And different discounts for next day and second day shipping. Many organizations are neglecting this critical factor in reducing freight charges.

This is especially so when it comes to comparing expedited, i.e. expensive, services. No wonder carriers want you to use their "free systems," which often bundle a "fair discount" in service, say ground shipping, with high-cost, high-profit rates in expedited services like next day air.

Fine-tuning, revisited. Rate shopping, as with other functions of the computerized shipping system, can be fine-tuned in several ways. Charges based on total order rating, for example, can be dramatically less than the sum of multiple packages calculated one-at-a-time. But your carrier might not volunteer this information; instead, it can be programmed into your system. (Chapter 13 discussed this principle earlier in more detail.) And watch out for special service fees, such as for hazardous materials, COD and declared value. If your system is not shopping based on the total charges, it could give you the wrong information.

Goal-processed shipping, the order of the day. Set up your rate shopping logic tree based on meeting this simple customer service issue: "When do you need to have the package?" Then, set-up rate shopping to compare the entire carrier's services that can meet that need. For example, if a customer needs his package in two days, compare ground rates as well as second day services.

There are many options available on a computerized shipping system that can solve different problems. Knowing what you want and specifying it will make it easier for you to do an "apples to apples" comparison. The next chapter will give you even more questions to ask your vendor. ◆

CHAPTER 19

Stand up and Deliver!

Ever look at the funny numbers on the backside of some manufactured product? Along with an inventory code or date of manufacture, there may be a reference to the purchaser's specifications. This is what I would like to address next, formally setting out specifications for your computerized shipping system. Detailing these deliverables, the concrete, measurable outputs of your shipping system, its implementation, and training will help ensure that you get the system you thought you paid for. Here's what to consider, ask about and expect.

Hardware. There's a lot to think about before booting up. Most computerized shipping systems will consist of a computer (PC), modem, scale, barcode scanner, report printer, and barcode label printer. You must ensure that your hardware has satisfactory capacity and compatibility for the intended shipping system. Important issues here include needed memory, monitor sizes, hard drive capacity, data backup, operating systems and modem compatibility. Make sure your vendor's hardware specifications are put down in writing. In this way, your MIS people or consultant can be sure your existing system is compatible with vendor-supplied items and can handle the intended functions. You now also have a delivery standard that can be verified if anything should go wrong. This is how we avoid those "It's your hardware's fault, not ours" or "I thought that was included" arguments which no one can really win.

Which carriers and services? The next deliverable to get in writing is a complete list of carriers and services that are to be included in your shipping system. Earlier, we talked about some of the different methods of processing packages with the carriers. For example, if you ship out International Air Small Packets with the U.S. Post Office, you want to make sure that your system incorporates that service. Furthermore, some carriers require that you install carrier-certified modules. Don't miss this step or you will end up not being able to ship or waiting for the carrier to make an exception. UPS lists its certified vendors, who they refer to as "on-line compatible," on their website: www.ups.com. Similarly, the USPS has its own vendor specification; what it calls a "MAC-Certified" module.

Interface—no time for fuzzy logic. You must know exactly what data fields are coming from your host system and what fields you want sent back. If it is to be on a network, you should know who is providing the network cards and file server and how the cabling will be done. Remember, when you decide to purchase or upgrade a computerized shipping system, you will also be conducting an analysis of your strategic business plan and capabilities. Often, this is the time to invest in an overall upgrade to your information business systems. Don't buy $300 shoes if you are still wearing $100 suits.

Although this book isn't meant to substitute for specialized knowledge in integration, I would like to briefly note the three most common ways of interfacing host business and shipping systems.

- **Terminal emulation;** also called screen mapping. This relatively simple method works by copying information from a screen in your accounting program and then sending it to the shipping system. The user "toggles" between applications such as we already do within programs in Microsoft Windows. Here's how it works: accounting and shipping applications will run on a single computer; the shipper brings up an order in your host system, presses a hot key, and the data is automatically transferred to the shipping application; after the package has been processed, data like the freight charges and tracking numbers is sent back to the host system — just as if an operator were typing it in. Nearly all systems can be interfaced this way, using software programs like ProComm Plus, Rumba, or Reflections to emulate computer terminals on IBM, DEC, HP, and just about any host computer that your company has.

- **ODBC;** which stands for Open Data Base Connectivity. It is commonly used to work with databases, such as Access, Microsoft SQL server and Oracle. You must know who will write the code or script that passes data between the two systems, as well as who is going to provide the ODBC drivers.
- **File Transfer;** this method transfers files electronically between your host and shipping systems, as we reviewed earlier in Chapters 5 and 6. It can be set up to function in real-time or files can be "held" and sent in batches. You must clarify data field layouts and file structure and how the data is to be moved from one system to the other. Typically, the host system exports the data to a

drive on a network. The shipping system can detect this file, process the shipment, and then send transaction data back to the host computer.

There are other ways to integrate systems, but the above methods are the most common. Most importantly, know which method your vendor is providing — and if it makes sense for your overall business system. This is where the MIS people earn their bread and butter.

System Output.

Getting it down and out on paper. Will your system be able to generate all required hard copy? The list of typical printouts is substantial and includes: packing lists and invoices; bar-coded tracking labels of the carriers you have selected; UCC128 container code labels or compliance labels required by your customers; special labels and bills of lading; carrier airbills and waybills; hazardous material tags; international export documents, such as shipper's export declaration (SED) forms and custom forms; and U. S. Post Office mailing statements and reports. Have these forms on hand for vendors to inspect, so you can accurately specify all expected output. For example, if you have USPS rates on your system, and you are manifesting your packages, the output you specify would include postage statements

3600-R, 3602-R, 3605-R and 3651-R. If you are including BAX Global, you want the Global Daily Remittance Report.

"Soft-put." Electronic transmissions and related items. Here, we must standardize and specify file formats for electronic data files (EDI), postage meter tapes, emails, faxes, even signals to control a conveyor. Almost all of the carriers have electronic shipment data files that must be electronically transmitted to them at the end of each shipping day. Your system must be able to fulfill each carrier's reporting standards.

Finally, be clear with your vendor regarding less-easy-to-define deliverables like installation, training and documentation. This is where costs can sometimes mysteriously mushroom. Make sure your contract defines days, costs, level of training and user manuals, and benchmarks to be met. For example, what about training of new employees? Who handles this and at what cost? Overall, I strongly believe in paying fairly for precisely defined services. Many "free-bees" never get used, while real charges soar on areas or responsibilities not properly defined in the first place. Chapter 21 provides some solid guidelines for smoothly implementing those deliverables.◆

CHAPTER 20

Where To Get A Computerized Shipping Solution: Making The Right Choice

When it comes to bringing your shipping operation "on-line," there are three distinct choices. You can order a "cookie cutter" system, try and develop your own, or work with a systems integrator – a Valued Added Reseller (VAR) that specializes in designing, installing and "bringing to speed" computerized shipping systems. In making your choice, consider such important issues as startup vs. long-term costs, the ability to "rate shop" different carriers, how the system interfaces with your firm's inventory and accounting systems, and overall adaptability and flexibility.

No Such Thing as a Free Cookie

Lured by prominent advertisements, many companies succumb to a cookie cutter approach. These systems, with their limited standard features, follow a "one size fits all" philosophy. You will find that such systems are built to limitations imposed by their manufacturer, not to the potential needs of your organization.

Cookie cutter systems are available from two main sources. First, there are those marketed by brand name corporations that sell a variety of other office products like copiers and mailing machines. Many times, if your old system is in the repair shop, the vendor can slip one of these in the shipping room and you can find yourself in a long-term lease without even knowing what happened. Second, there are the "free" systems offered by the package carriers. In the majority of cases, this is the most expensive solution because, as discussed in detail in Chapter 16, such "free" systems are usually provided in lieu of giving additional rate discounts.

In either case, it is easy to get mesmerized by a brand name – and the sheer size of the sales force that markets the system, making us less than objective when assessing capabilities and real costs.

Unfortunately, cookie cutter systems lack flexibility and perpetrate wasteful shipping practices. Equipment vendors that are interested in moving their product out of inventory sell them and then it's on to the next prospect. Like the "free" systems from the carriers, these brand name systems offer the lowest common denominator of features.

Furthermore, they are usually serviced by the same technicians who service a company's mailing and copying equipment; they have little or no training in computers. Don't expect these technicians to have any real interest or ability in analyzing your current shipping practices. And if it is one of the "free" systems, don't expect the carrier to program it to handle other carriers or even shop for the least expensive rate within its own package delivery system. Therein lay some of the hidden costs of such "free" systems.

I'll Do It Myself?

Out of frustration and bad experiences, some companies decide to write their own "in-house" shipping system. This approach can provide the customization that an organization needs, and, initially, may appear to be a less expensive solution.

In practice, however, a company can find itself straining valuable programming and MIS resources in an area where they lack the shipping experience to do the job right. United Parcel Service, FedEx, and the other carriers are constantly introducing new services, discounts, and rate structures. It would require a full time staff to stay abreast of the changes. A company could miss significant profit opportunities because they did not have the time or expertise to research the latest discount programs. Again, there are hidden costs to doing-it-yourself.

Specialist Help

The third source for computerizing your shipping operation is your local VAR or systems integrator, a true specialist in computerized shipping systems. Most employ engineers with college degrees in electrical engineering or computer science that can customize your system to your organization's precise needs. More importantly, their owners and staff have dedicated their careers to this industry. As such, they have accumulated many years of practical experience and knowledge of how other shippers have solved problems and saved on freight.

Generally, they are committed not only to selling you a piece of hardware they have in stock, but to providing you with a total shipping solution that meets your firm's current needs and anticipates its future ones. Of course, not all VARs are the same. You will have to research references and judge their expertise and competence.

Salespeople from the office equipment vendors will suggest that because many reputable and competent VARs are not major national companies, you face the risk that the VAR could go out of business, leaving you "stranded." They conveniently forget to mention that large companies can also drop product lines and leave their customers without support.

The majority of VARs supply non-proprietary computers that can easily be replaced, upgraded, and serviced by standard PC providers. Fortune 500 companies like Standard Register Company, General Electric and Unisys have selected VARs, to provide computerized shipping systems. They have earned their confidence and can be trusted to be around in the future.

The Bottom Line

To summarize, there are advantages and risks with each type of computerized shipping vendor. The difference is you should choose a vendor who acts as a true consultant; one who analyzes your present shipping operation; interviews your staff on its current practices and needs; and designs a system that provides the most productive and cost effective solutions to your requirements.

Your vendor of choice should come up with ideas that can save you thousands of dollars a month. They should be experienced in integrating shipping systems into accounting systems and reengineering your shipping department to utilize leading edge technology, improving productivity — and profits. When the long-term savings throughout an organization are calculated, selecting the right vendor is often the most cost-effective solution. ◆

CHAPTER 21

Proper Planning and Preparation Essential in Controlling Total Costs

GET A RUNNING START ON IMPLEMENTATION

Let's face it, back in the days of the Pyramids or the Great Churches of Europe, the cost of materials, no matter how enormous, was a tiny proportion of the total expense for these mind-boggling, grand expressions of our human spirit. Just think what coffee breaks must have cost in those scenarios!

Flash forward many centuries. Whether it's an automotive assembly line or the computer network in a small business, we have learned, sometimes painfully, that the costs of implementation involve much more than the costs of the hardware. In modern lingo, we must understand, plan for and control both the physical and human infrastructures for any new business system. The same principle applies to computerized shipping systems. Just as I have emphasized throughout this book the importance of smart "buying;" now I want to emphasize and discuss the right way to implement a new system — once the purchase decision has been made.

I've seen it happen all too often. The purchase decision is made, the vendor order goes out and then key managers let their guard down, waiting for it all to happen, magically, on delivery day.

Many companies spend a lot of time selecting a computerized shipping system vendor, but once the purchase order has been issued, don't do a thing until the system shows up at their door. The gap between ordering and implementation can be costly in terms of startup confusion, downtime as kinks in the system get worked out, errors and delays in shipping schedules, lost employee time and lost productivity, and, worst of all, customer dissatisfaction. In effect, this could wipe out the savings realized by purchasing the "right" system for your organization.

These disruptions can cost as much as $2,000 per day in additional, unforeseen expenses. Instead, here are five key steps to planning and preparing for the installation of your new system, before it arrives at the door, that can substantially reduce the emotional and dollar costs of getting your new system up and running.

1. **Select a project manager.** It is a major undertaking to set up a computerized shipping system that can do all the "good stuff," including integrating with your host computer business system in such areas as inventory, billing and quality assurance, while also letting you choose the "best buy" among multiple carriers. It calls for close coordination between your information services (IS or MIS department), accounting, shipping, purchasing, and management, plus your accounting system vendor and any outside professional consultants. Computers may have to be purchased and networks installed, or existing networks double-checked. You may need to sign your contracts with the carriers and do preliminary work like develop sample labels and perform electronic transmission tests. If all this can take place in a planned and orderly fashion, you can have a smooth implementation. If a vendor has to play phone tag and get stuck in voice mail jail with multiple people within your own company, it could become ugly. The best path to success: put a project manager in charge of this

coordination and give her or him the authority to make decisions and get things done right.

2. **Hold the pickles and mayo.** Know exactly what you want in advance. You have already pre-identified the carriers and services you would utilize in the systems analysis and purchasing phases. Now, we're getting down to the nitty-gritty. How will you process C.O.D. shipments? Are you going to impose handling charges; if so, how much and under what circumstances? How are you going to identify collect versus prepaid shipments? When do you use declared value or the carrier's insurance? What are the carrier codes or "ship vias" that your order entry people will use? There are many fine nuances to the smooth operation of a computerized shipping department. You must have the shipping process defined like a blueprint for a house, with specific protocols that help ensure efficiency, error-free operation and uniform treatment of all customers. Furthermore, these design details must be communicated clearly to your vendor, because changes — in-house or with your vendor — are expensive.
3. **Identify a key operator.** Far too often, training is conducted haphazardly; maybe, right in the

warehouse with your operator being constantly interrupted. Many times, companies decide that the entire shipping department should be trained in the use of a computerized shipping system. While this may be a noble objective, at least at first, it is much easier to train a single user well than it is to train many people to a level of minimum competence. You are much better off having a competent lead operator that can train the rest of your staff. Make sure that this person knows in advance that he or she will be assuming this responsibility (and explain how important it is) and make sure they are available for training. It is often helpful to get a user's manual to this person for study before actual training with your vendor. Choose someone with a knack for computers in general, real competency at your host computer and its operating system, and the motivation and intelligence to succeed in a self-starting, Total Quality Management and innovation environment. These people are out there, right in your own organization. But take nothing for granted here; we have spent days at sites just getting the assigned operator up to speed on basic computer use. If the person is right from an overall talent and motivation standpoint, but lacks those basic computer skills, get them trained in advance of I-day; (implementation day).

4. **Don't forget the keys.** You must have information services (IS) support available. Ever rush out the front door when the kids come home from school, anxious to show off the new family car, but forget and leave the keys on the dining room table? I am almost embarrassed to tell you how much time has been lost at individual companies on I-day because no one was available that knew the password into the host system. A shipping system vendor is not an expert in your accounting software and host hardware. If you are connecting systems, then have those people present who understand the system to which you are connecting. If you are to provide the computers, ensure that they are configured to specification and functioning before the vendor's implementation team arrives. Your network administrator (if that is someone different from the IS officer) should also be accessible. Have some dummy orders available for testing before you begin shipping. Taylor's Law says that Murphy was an optimist. You don't want to waste time chasing down the only people that know how to fix the problem.

5. **Make room.** Where is the shipping system going to be placed? What are you going to put it on? Not that rickety old table in the corner. A quality, modern computerized shipping system and department calls for a modern environment; including a workstation that has been ergonomically designed with the keyboard and monitor at the right height. How about a fatigue mat for your operator that has to stand there? Are there enough electrical outlets; with clean power and grounded? What about surge protection and backup battery power supply? Do you have a dedicated telephone line in place for the modem that will communicate between your computerized shipping system and your carriers? Is the terminal or network line working? Test it out in advance. Again, we don't want to waste expensive engineer, MIS or vendor time because of such oversights. Like computerized shipping systems in general, it's all in the details.

Overall, as I have indicated, poor planning can lead to expensive delays, wasted time and money, and staff and customer dissatisfaction. We don't want to lose the confidence of all those staff who have been "sold" on the impending benefits of your new or upgraded computerized shipping system. Be sure to get off on your strongest possible shipping foot; then the computerized shipping system will be a welcome pleasure to everyone involved. No frowns or laughs behind the key management's back, just smiles. ◆

CHAPTER 22

Computerized Shipping System Case Study 1: Merle Distributing Company

In operation for over 30 years, Redford, Michigan-based Merle Distributing Company is known as a "jobber" in the book distribution industry. The firm, which was purchased by former bank executive John Buell in March of 1990, provides its customers – major bookstore chains, libraries and schools – quick turnaround on a large, diverse inventory. If a store wants a popular or "hot" book for its shelves within 24 hours, Merle services that need.

With a 15,000-square foot facility and 20 employees, Merle Distributing ships between 150-300 packages a day from January to September. During the holiday season (October through December) 400 to 600 packages a day are shipped.

Formerly, Merle's operating procedure for the movement of inventory was for books to be boxed according to telemarketers' invoices. Separately, package labels were generated. Manually, the package labels and invoices had to be matched.

On average, two daily man-hours were spent matching labels and invoices. Not only was this process inefficient, but errors also resulted in misdeliveries.

"If we were hitting 85 percent (of our deliveries), we were doing well," said Buell. "We had severe problems."

Misdeliveries meant unsatisfied customers. In turn, Merle Distributing had to service these customers and assume the costs of tracing and reshipping the misdelivered packages.

Having an employee spend over a half-day from January to September and a full day during the holiday season solely on adding the freight charges to the invoices was a significant commitment of wasted resources for a company of Merle's size.

"Sometimes during the holiday season, the person closing the invoices would get behind, requiring two people to close the invoices," Buell remembers. "It was a horror show."

Looking to ship in a more cost-effective and accurate manner, Merle Distributing sought the help of technology, installing a computerized shipping system.

The computerized shipping system automates the parcel shipping process and is fully interfaced with the company's business system to reduce labor and the costly errors associated with manual processing.

Being able to interface the computerized shipping system with his business system was the selling point for Buell. Merle's business system operates with Pick software on an Altos Computer. Interfacing the two without major programming problems was thought to be nearly impossible by Merle management.

Instead of creating new problems and challenges, this user-friendly system eliminated Merle's old problems instantly as its shipping department was transformed from a problem center into a profit center. Employee training on the new system was minimal.

"It was probably the smartest investment we ever made," Buell said. "The system paid for itself in six months."

Merle's telemarketers generate the inventory picking slips, which are bar coded using Code 128 symbology. When it comes time to ship, a shipping clerk places the parcel on an electronic scale. A scanning gun shoots the bar code to call up the customer, and the invoice is created. Simultaneously, the thermal transfer printer prints a single label with the ship-to-address and carrier's bar code. Once the package is shipped, the invoice is automatically closed in the company's business system, with the freight charges added.

In the office and warehouse, the wasted time and errors that come with manual processing were eliminated. Not only was the system more cost-efficient internally, it also was more effective. Misdeliveries dropped to one percent. The customer service department literally vanished. After misdeliveries were eliminated, service could be upgraded. Buell is happy to report that there have been no problems whatsoever with the computerized shipping system.

In this age of multiple delivery carriers, Merle can offer its customers the delivery system of its choice through the computerized shipping system. Also, multiple orders from the same customer are conveniently grouped into one package. On packages for which Merle assumes the freight charges, the computerized shipping system automatically shops for the best rates.

Bottom line, the computerized shipping system keeps the flow in the warehouse uninterrupted – a key for any efficient shipping department.

"We have a totally automated system," Buell said. "We are out of the '70s, operating the way a growing corporation should be." ◆

CHAPTER 23

Computerized Shipping System Case Study 2: Servall

Based in Centerline, Michigan (suburban Detroit), Servall is among the country's top appliance parts distributors; counting among its suppliers such industry heavyweights as Amana, Frigidaire, General Electric, Maytag and Whirlpool.

Founded in 1929, this third generation company today has 14 facilities located throughout the mid-west and northeast, including Michigan, Ohio and Indiana. Servall ships more than 700,000 lbs. of product via one million packages a year, generating annual revenues in excess of $18 million.

Kim Adler, president of Servall, recognized the growing significance of e-commerce and realized it would soon impact the competitive position of distributorships; the traditional “”middleperson” of the

American economy. His goal: a pre-emptive strike on the competition, designed to increase shipping efficiency, cost savings and promote corporate growth. Once again, this is an example of how the decision to purchase or upgrade a computerized shipping system can transcend the shipping room.

The system included hardware and software that allowed for bar code scanning of work orders; automatic rate shopping among the major carriers; thermal printing of shipping labels; laser printing of packing lists; automatic tracking of packages; interfacing of all data with the Servall accounting system; and a service to detect and calculate refunds for a carrier's self-imposed delivery standards that were not met.

The benefits were immediate and substantial and continue to grow to this day. They include:

- **Lower Labor Costs.** By eliminating most manual labor tasks (i.e. keystroking of data, package labeling, fielding of customer calls regarding package tracking), Servall was immediately able to cut its shipping room staff by 2 persons, resulting in net savings per year of $50,000 to $60,000 in labor costs.
- **Lower Materials Costs.** The old packing list system, with its costly pre-printed shop-type forms, was eliminated, replaced by a laser printer.

Even after the cost of laser printing was calculated, Servall realized savings here of $200 a day, about $50,000 per year.

- **Lower Insurance Costs.** Prior to utilizing the new computerized shipping system, Servall was shipping with a "free" UPS-provided system. As a result, Servall paid insurance costs on packages as dictated by this carrier alone of $0.35 per $100 of package value after the first $100 of value. By being able to self-insure its packages, Servall is saving as much as $1,500 a month, or $18,000 each year.
- **Ability to Invoice More Efficiently.** By interfacing shipping with the company's accounting system, invoices are generated and mailed up to a day sooner than before. Generally, faster collection means fewer draws on a company's existing credit line, saving interest charges. A recent analysis in INC. magazine demonstrated that savings can be calculated by the following formula: Gross annual sales x annual interest rate x days saved = dollar savings /365. For Servall, the math went like this: $18 million x .09% x 1 day saved/365 = $5,000/year.
- **Getting Rid of Mistakes.** By eliminating the stand alone shipping system and getting an integrated system that always has the correct

address, Servall has been able to eliminate costly mistakes at many steps in the shipping and accounting process. Consider: Industry accepted standards in this area state that the average cost of a mistake that needs to be corrected is approximately $50. Prior to implementing the new computerized shipping system, Servall estimates it was making approximately 300 mistakes per month. Subsequent to utilizing the new technology, mistakes dropped to 35 a month, even though volumes had more than doubled, to 12,000 orders a month. Thus, 265 mistakes were eliminated per month. Even at $25 per mistake, the monthly savings equals $6,625, or $80,000 each year.

- **Freight Savings.** I mentioned Servall had been utilizing a "free" computerized shipping system supplied by UPS. With such systems, a shipper is basically at the mercy of the carrier supplying the technology; as it does not rate shop whatsoever among the major carriers. You can only ship with that one carrier. With the new system, Servall was soon in a better position (with more information at its disposal with regard to rates/discounts of all major carriers) to negotiate a greater discount from UPS. Servall was able to realize an additional

$77,000/year in freight savings. (So, was their carrier system really free?)

Two years later, Servall continues on its strong growth course. The company's shipping volumes have more than quadrupled, from 200 to 800 packages per day, while its computerized shipping system is saving Servall $300,000 each year in shipping expense, freeing valuable capital for growth.

Notes Servall president Kim Adler, "If you don't watch shipping costs, they can become a silent killer. We have transformed our shipping room from a cost center into a true, tangible profit center." ◆

Conclusion

This book has introduced a myriad of possibilities that a computerized shipping system can offer to virtually any organization. I have described how to transform a shipping department from a 'cost center' to a 'profit center.' Shipping departments truly have the means by which they can enjoy increased control, productivity, simplicity, accuracy and speed with less hassle and costly mistakes. Management, meanwhile, can more effectively achieve such strategic objectives as lowering costs, improving customer service, increasing productivity, offering new flexibility, reducing errors and providing a vital communications link through a finely orchestrated technological system.

I have provided options to operations and shipping managers as to the capabilities that are available and the sources from which a computerized shipping system can be acquired. I have suggested a careful and prudent examination of the motives and competency of the providers of computerized shipping systems.

For salespeople, I hope that this book is utilized as a valuable training tool. I have described how to cost justify a system for a prospective client. I have pointed out the challenges that shipping and operations managers must deal with on a daily basis. I have detailed the inherent problems caused by carriers providing "free systems." Most importantly, I hope that this book has demonstrated the importance of personal integrity and properly educating the customer. This technology truly can make a difference — on many different levels; eliminating mindless errors while increasing national competitiveness. As the economist Paul Zane Pilzer said,

> *"What accounts for progress? That is, how has humanity managed to improve its way of life over the millennia? At its most basic level, the answer involves technology. Very simply, the world has progressed by finding and implementing better ways of doing things."*

Salespeople have historically been directly responsible for the implementation of technology and the progress of society. I am proud to have been a part of it.

Mark A. Taylor
Detroit
2000

About The Author

Mark Taylor is president and CEO of TAYLOR Systems Engineering Corporation, a Plymouth, Michigan-based consulting and engineering company specializing in computerized shipping systems. Over the past 25 years, Taylor has combined sales savvy, a fascination with personal computers and an intense desire to own his own company, to form one of the most successful private companies in the state of Michigan.

A product of humble beginnings in the downriver community of Taylor, Michigan, he garnered many scholarships and academic honors during high school. Taylor spent 13 years with Pitney Bowes, distinguishing himself as both a salesperson and sales manager during his tenure. During his last seven years with the company, he ranked in the top five percent of all sales representatives and all sales managers nationwide.

While working for Pitney Bowes, Taylor also earned his Bachelor's degree in computers and management from William James College. Ever alert to new technologies and business trends, he immediately recognized the potential of personal computers to reduce workloads and errors. He introduced personal computers to the company, automating sales reports and producing trend studies. Taylor's mangers were so impressed with his work, in fact, that when it came time to deploy a computerized parcel shipping system, the job was his.

About that time, Taylor noticed important changes occurring in the business arena. Companies of all sizes were looking to reduce expenses and cut overhead. Every department became a candidate for streamlining. All, it seemed, except shipping. Shipping departments were often "out back," out-of-sight places where few outside staff (let alone cost-cutters), ventured. A company's shipping costs were often simply tacked-on to customer invoices. Since the customer paid for freight, few explored the option of turning the shipping department into a 'profit center.'

Seizing upon the immense corporate need for computerization to provide rapid, cost-effective and accurate parcel shipping, Taylor formed his own company, TAYLOR Systems Engineering Corporation. He met with shipping room managers and demonstrated how any company shipping 50 or more packages a day stood to reduce costs and improve cash flow by adopting his program. He staffed TAYLOR Systems Engineering Corporation with professionally degreed engineers, an innovation that assured his clients complete analysis, specification, design and engineering services. By helping customers select the cheapest parcel carrier, generate accurate labels, and interface the shipping and accounting departments, Taylor successfully "moved" shipping from a back room 'cost center' to an envied 'profit center.'

Today, TAYLOR Systems Engineering Corporation's impressive client roster includes such business heavyweights as Michelin Tire, Unisys and Standard Register Corporation. In 1995, TAYLOR Systems Engineering Corporation was named to the prestigious "Michigan Private 100," an honor accorded the fastest growing companies in the state of Michigan.

From 1993 to 1998, Taylor further honed his business skills by attending the University of Phoenix during the evenings; he received his Masters in Business Administration in June 1998.

In a career spanning more than two decades, Taylor estimates he has consulted more than 10,000 organizations on increasing profit and productivity. He is the creator of ***www.shippingrefunds.com,*** the revolutionary technology that helps shippers obtain refunds on guaranteed packages that the carrier has failed to deliver on time.

Considered one of the nation's leading authorities on computerized shipping systems, Taylor is frequently asked to speak at national industry conventions. His insights can also be found regularly in leading business and industry trade publications.

He resides with his wife and family in suburban Detroit.

Glossary

3 Day Select

An UPS service that guarantees delivery within three business days throughout the 48 contiguous states; electronic package tracing is included.

Account Number

(See also: "shipper number") Number assigned by carriers to identify a shipper for billing purposes. This number appears on the manifest, package label, and pickup record book.

AI

(Artificial Intelligence).

Airbill

A document used by airfreight carriers acknowledging receipt of goods and agreeing to transport them to a consignee.

Airborne

Short for Airborne Express, an express delivery carrier based out of Seattle, Washington. (www.airborne.com)

Algorithm

A finite number of steps, following a set of defined rules, for the solution to a problem or the completion of a task.

AOD

(Acknowledgment of Delivery) Special service offered by carriers requiring a consignee to sign a receipt (AOD card), a copy of which is returned to the shipper as proof of delivery.

ASCII

(American Standard Code for Information Interchange) A character set or code established by the American National Standards Institute (ANSI) to achieve compatibility between data services. It is commonly used for importing and exporting data.

Bar Code

An automated identification technology that encodes information into an array of varying width parallel rectangle bars and spaces. Used for automated data input via a bar code wand or scanner. Types of bar codes include 39, Interleave 2 of 5, Codabar, 128, UPC, etc.

Batch Processing

A group of records that are "batched" or pooled for entry at a single time.

BAX Global

Formerly known as Burlington. A carrier based out of Irvine, California. (www.baxglobal.com)

Baud

Refers to the speed of computer communications in bits per second.

Bit

Short for Binary Digit; the lowest logical element used by a computer.

Bitmap

An image stored as a pattern of dots.

BOL

(Bill of Lading) A document created by the shipper that contains the carrier's name, consignor, consignee, # of units, article description, weight and class.

Boot

A term for starting up the computer.

Byte

A unit of computer memory, about the size of a single character.

Calibration

The process used to bring a scale into specification.

Call Tag

Special service offered by carriers which authorizes a carrier to pick up a shipment from another location and bring it to the shipper's location.

Character

A single number, letter, or punctuation.

Class or Classification

Refers to Freight Classification, a classification set forth by the Uniform Freight Classification Chart that categorizes goods shipped in terms of value, size, weight, and density.

COD

(Collect on Delivery) Special service offered by carriers whereby a shipper authorizes a driver to collect a designated amount of money from a consignee as a condition of delivery.

Codabar

A numeric-only bar code, in which each number is represented by seven black and white bars.

***Code* 39**

A full alphanumeric bar code consisting of nine black and white bars for each character symbol.

***Code* 128**

A full alphanumeric bar code capable of encoding all 128 ASCII characters.

Common Carrier

A company in the business of transporting goods or merchandise for a fee.

Consignee

The receiver of shipped goods; the ship-to destination.

Consignee Billing

A method of sending packages where the consignee has to pay for the freight.

Consignor

The company shipping goods.

Conveyor Controller

A programmable device that is used to control the operation of a conveyor.

CSR

(Customer Service Representative)

Database

A large collection of data that is organized. An address book is a database. Software programs like Microsoft's Access are used to electronically collect data.

Declared Value

The value or worth of the contents of a package that is declared on a manifest for insurance purposes.

DHL

An express carrier mostly known for international shipping. (www.dhl.com)

Dimensional Weight

A standard formula used by delivery companies to measure a package's density. Applies to air service shipments that measure more than one cubic foot and that, according to the formula, are considered large in proportion to their weight.

Diskette

A removable disk media; sometimes called a floppy (because they used to be).

Docu-Label

Label printed by computerized shipping system bearing shipping information to be adhered to shipper's documentation (instead of a document printer).

Document Printer

Printing device used by computerized shipping systems to print shipping information (shipping charges, weight, carrier, etc.) on a shipper's internal documentation (shipping papers, invoice, packing slip, etc.)

DOS

(Disk Operating System) Term used to describe standard software used on IBM compatible personal computers to allow run application software programs to run. DOS is a set of programs that instruct the PC as to scheduling, supervision, control, and management of the computer's resources.

Dot Matrix

Method of printing involving an impression created via a ballistic pin configuration and ink ribbon film.

Downloading

The transfer of data from a host computer into the shipping computer. The same as import.

Drop Ship

Method used by a shipper whereby a shipment is priced and manifested by a computerized shipping system as if it were processed at a different location. This method is used to reduce shipping charges by taking advantage of a more favorable zone/pricing structure.

EDI

(Electronic Data Interchange) Transfer of data; within the context of shipment processing allows shippers to transmit manifest information electronically to carriers for billing and tracing purposes.

Emery

Short for Emery Worldwide. An express carrier. (www.emeryworld.com)

Export

Data transmitted from a shipping computer to a disk or computer, typically includes the freight charges & tracking number.

FedEx

Carrier based in Memphis, TN known for air shipments. Acquired RPS (Roadway Package Systems) and renamed it FedEx Ground. (www.fedex.com)

FedEx Ground

Packages sent by ground service. Previously known as RPS. (www.fedexground.com)

Field

A piece of information which forms a part of a transaction or record. The phone number could be a field in an address book database.

File

A number of records organized as a unit, usually sharing a common value. The address book could be a file.

File Server

The hard drive of a network that collects all the data from the work stations. Usually it is a separate computer with a large disk capacity.

Floppy Disk

The removable disk used to store data.

F.O.B. Destination Freight Collect and Allowed

Buyer pays freight charges, but seller bears freight charges and owns goods in transit.

F.O.B. Destination, Freight Collect

Buyer pays and bears freight charges, but seller owns goods in transit.

F.O.B.

(Free On Board)

F.O.B. Origin, Freight Collect

Buyer pays freight charges, bears freight charges, and owns goods in transit.

F.O.B. Origin, Freight Prepaid

Seller pays and bears freight charges, but buyer owns goods in transit.

F.O.B. Origin, Freight Prepaid and Charged Back

Seller pays freight charges, but buyer bears freight charges and owns goods in transit.

F.O.B. Destination, Freight Prepaid

Seller pays and bears freight charges and also owns goods in transit.

Hard Disk

Non-removable disk media used to store large amounts of data.

Hardware

The equipment, like the PC, label printer, and scale.

Host Computer

The main computer a company utilizes to run its order entry, inventory, and accounting system.

Hundred Weight

Service offered by UPS whereby packages designated for a destination are rated according to aggregate weight instead of individual weight.

ICC

(Interstate Commerce Commission)

Import

Data transmitted from another computer (typically the host computer) to be utilized by the shipping computer. Typically includes the consignee address information, zip code and service level.

Interstate

Parcel shipment service and shipping rates for parcels shipped from one state to another.

Intrastate

Parcel shipment service and shipping rates for parcels shipped to and from locations in the same state.

JIT

(Just In Time) Shipping goods just before they are needed to reduce inventory overhead.

LAN

(Local Area Network) A high-speed data communications architecture facilitating the sharing of resources (files, databases) and devices (printers, hard disks, PCs).

Laser Scanner

Non-contact bar code reading device (see also: Wand).

Lightpen

In a bar code system, a hand-held scanning wand that is used as a contact bar code reader. It is the size and shape of a pen.

Live Communication

Real time, on-line communication between the shipping computer and the host computer.

LTL

(Less Than Load) Generic term usually used to refer to shipments made by a carrier other than package carriers such as UPS or FedEx, usually freight carriers such as Yellow Freight or Roadway that will rate a shipment based on class, total weight, etc.

Mainframe Computer

A large-scale closed architecture computer normally supplied with all peripherals and hardware by a single large vendor.

Manifest

Report approved by a specific carrier that itemizes and totals package weights and charges in a format suitable for billing, claims, and auditing purposes.

Megabyte

One million bytes.

MIS

(Management Information System) The MIS group within a corporation is responsible for operating and maintaining all computer-related devices, software, and databases.

Modem

Device used to enable computers to communicate with other computers.

Module

A software unit that performs one or more functions. A module on a computerized shipping system might provide the ability to ship with another carrier.

Mouse

A pointing device used to control cursor movement.

Multi-user Network

A shipping system with multiple work stations, with one such station being used as a file server that collects totals from all the others.

Multi-Weight

Service offered by FedEx Ground (formerly RPS) whereby packages designated for a destination are rated according to aggregate weight instead of individual weight.

Node

Point of interconnection to a network; a LAN work station.

ODBC

(Open Data Base Connectivity) It is a means of interfacing to a database.

On-line Processing

(Also Real Time Communication) Live communication between computers on a transaction by transaction basis.

Oversize

Special service offered by carriers enabling shippers to ship a package that exceeds certain maximum size requirements.

Package ID Number

Unique number assigned by a shipper to identify a particular package. It is usually an invoice, order, customer, or any other number that will ultimately identify a consignee name and address. The number is used for auditing, tracing, and claims purposes.

Packer

The individual who places merchandise into containers, and seals and labels them prior to weighing and calculation of the shipping charge.

Parallel Communication

Method of communication used by a computer to communicate with a peripheral device (usually a printer) via a “parallel port”. Parallel ports are normally referred to as “LPT1”, “LPT2” and “LPT3”. (See also Serial Communication). Communication occurs a byte at a time with each bit transmitted simultaneously over parallel lines.

PC

Term used to describe an IBM compatible Personal Computer, usually with a Pentium processor.

PDI

(Package Data Interchange) High-volume shippers can take advantage of PDI to collect and transfer package information directly to the FedEx computer system through a modem.

Picker

The person who obtains merchandise from manufacturing or inventory for shipment. He or she uses the invoice or shipping memo as a guide in picking the merchandise.

Pickup Record Book

A logbook provided by a package carrier such as UPS which contains pages sequentially numbered for identification purposes. When a shipment is ready for pickup by a carrier, the shipper writes the accumulated totals appearing at the end of the manifest into the corresponding areas of the current pickup record page. A copy of the page is then affixed to the manifest that is taken with the shipment. The shipper keeps the other copy.

Pickup Record Number

Number assigned by a package carrier, such as UPS, to identify a particular shipment/manifest. This number appears sequentially in the upper right corner of each page of the pickup record book. The number is also printed by computerized shipping system in the heading of each page of the manifest.

PIP

(Private Insurance Plan) An alternative to carrier's declared value parcel insurance offered by a third party insurer.

POD

(Proof of Delivery) POD's include the date a package was delivered and the name and signature of the person who signed for the package.

Powership Plus

A method of package processing developed by third parties approved by FedEx for billing purposes. It includes routing and electronically transmitting package data through a modem.

Prepay & Add

Freight is paid by the sender & then added to the invoice to the receiver.

Pro Number

Number used to identify LTL shipment on Bill of Lading.

Processor

Computer component used to process data. PC systems use Pentium processors manufactured by Intel Corp.

Program

A set of instructions for a computer. A shipping application is also known as a program. Also a verb, meaning to create the instructions, as in to program the computer.

Protocol Converter

A device that translates one communication protocol to another, such as IBM SNA/SDLC to ASCII.

QWERTY

The standard keyboard configuration as seen on typewriters and computer terminals.

Real-Time Communication

Live communication between computers on a transaction by transaction basis.

RPS

(Roadway Package System); package carrier. Acquired by FedEx and known as FedEx Ground. (www.fedex.com)

RS-232

An EIA standard for connecting data processing devices usually limited in distance to 50 feet.

RTV

(Return to Vendor) FedEx Ground program that is similar to a call tag.

Scanner

An electronic device to read bar codes that electro-optically converts bars and spaces into electrical signals.

Serial Communication

Method of communication used by a computer to communicate with another device via a "serial port". Serial ports are normally described as "COM1", "COM2", "COM3", etc. (See also Parallel Communication). Serial communication is characterized by the transmission of data one bit at a time down a communication line or channel.

SED

(Shipper's Export Declaration) It is a form used for shipping internationally.

Ship VIA

The method or level of service desired by the customers. Examples would be Ground, Second Day, Next day, Priority, Express, or LTL.

Shipper Number

(Also "Account Number") Number assigned by carriers to identify a shipper for billing purposes. This number appears on the manifest, package label, and pickup record book.

Shipping

The preparation of merchandise for shipment to customers. The packing, labeling and calculation of shipping charges, and transferring to a carrier.

Shipping Labels

Document attached to parcel giving name and address of sender and consignee. May also list contents of parcel.

Special Services

Service offered by a carrier, beyond the standard contract of carriage, for which an additional charge applies. Declared Value is a special service.

Stand Alone Systems

Shipping systems that are not interfaced into a host computer.

SWOG

(Ship With Other Goods) Term refers to procedure whereby multiple orders are packed within a master container.

Terminal Emulation

Software designed to enable a PC computer to "look" like an on-line terminal to a host computer.

Thermal Label Printing

Method of label printing whereby special label stock (thermal label) is heated to cause an impression. Conventional ink and ink ribbons are not used in this method. ("Thermal transfer" is a method of thermal printing which involves the heating of a thermal ribbon on to label stock.

Tracking Number

Number assigned by a package carrier, such as UPS, Airborne, and FedEx, to identify individual packages. The number is usually bar coded and used by carriers to trace the package through their distribution system. It can also be used to trace packages on the World Wide Web at the carrier's website.

Transaction

A record, which contains all information (weight, charges, carrier, etc.), related to a particular package.

UPC

(Universal Product Code) The standard bar code symbol for retail packages in the United States.

Upload

Data transmitted from the shipping computer to the host computer. The same as export.

UPS

(United Parcel Service); A package carrier, based in Atlanta, GA. (www.ups.com)

USPS

(United States Postal Service) Famous for delivering the mail; carrier that has Express Mail for overnight delivery and Priority mail. (www.usps.gov)

VAR

(Value Added Reseller) A company that sells a software package developed by a third party and adds value such as implementation & training.

Vendor Supplied System

A manifest system provided by a third party, typically a VAR or systems integrator.

Wand Scanner

A hand-held scanning device used as a contact bar code.

Wand

Contact bar code reading device (see also Laser Scanner).

WMS

(Warehouse Management System) A program that automates a warehouse, usually the receiving and picking processes.

Worldwide Express

An UPS service, which provides delivery of documents, packages, and letters internationally. Shipments are typically delivered within two days.

Worldwide Expedited

An UPS service which provides scheduled delivery of airfreight packages to major trading countries. Shipments are typically delivered in four business days.

WYSIWYG

"What you see, is what you get" method for designing and printing graphics.

Zone Skipping

When a shipper trucks his packages across a couple of zones & then drops them off at a carrier distribution site.

Zone

Value assigned by a carrier to describe a geographical position relative to the origin of a shipment.

For more information, questions or additional copies of this book, contact:

Director/Educational Services
Angelico & Taylor Inc.
40800 Five Mile Road
Plymouth, MI 48170

Phone:	(734) 420-7447
Fax:	(734) 420-7460
E-Mail:	mtaylor@shippingsys.com
Website:	www.shippingsys.com